D1609695

HUMAN RIGHTS AND EQUALITY IN EDUCATION

Comparative perspectives on the right to education for minorities and disadvantaged groups

Edited by Sandra Fredman, Meghan Campbell and Helen Taylor

First published in Great Britain in 2018 by

Policy Press
University of Bristol
1-9 Old Park Hill
Bristol
BS2 8BB
UK
t: +44 (0)117 954 5940
pp-info@bristol.ac.uk
www.policypress.co.uk

North America office:
Policy Press
c/o The University of Chicago Press
1427 East 60th Street
Chicago, IL 60637, USA
t: +1 773 702 7700
f: +1 773-702-9756
sales@press.uchicago.edu
www.press.uchicago.edu

© Policy Press 2018

British Library Cataloguing in Publication Data
A catalogue record for this book is available from the British Library

Library of Congress Cataloging-in-Publication Data
A catalog record for this book has been requested

ISBN 978-1-4473-3763-8 hardcover
ISBN 978-1-4473-3765-2 ePub
ISBN 978-1-4473-3766-9 Mobi
ISBN 978-1-4473-3764-5 epdf

The right of Sandra Fredman, Meghan Campbell and Helen Taylor to be identified as editors
of this work has been asserted by them in accordance with the Copyright, Designs and
Patents Act 1988.

Cover design by Policy Press
Front cover image: UN photo database
Printed and bound in Great Britain by CPI Group (UK) Ltd,
Croydon, CR0 4YY
Policy Press uses environmentally responsible print partners

Contents

Notes on contributors

Michael Bishop is in-house counsel at the Constitutional Litigation Unit of the Legal Resources Centre (LRC). He has appeared in the Constitutional Court, the Supreme Court of Appeal, the High Court and the Land Claims Court on issues including customary law, education, freedom of expression, refugee rights, environmental law, land rights, gender equality, housing, administrative law and social security. He has a particular interest in issues relating to openness and accountability. Prior to joining the LRC, Michael worked in a variety of legal advisory and legal research roles including two years clerking for Chief Justice Pius Langa. Michael has also taught constitutional law and administrative law to LLM students at the University of Pretoria, the University of Cape Town and the National Law University in New Delhi. He is currently an Honorary Research Associate at the Department of Public Law at UCT. Michael is the Managing Editor of the leading text on South African constitutional law, Woolman's *Constitutional Law of South Africa*, for which he has also authored several chapters. Together with Jason Brickhill, Khomotso Moshikaro and Meghan Finn he authors the constitutional law updates for *Juta's Quarterly Review* and the *Annual Survey of South African Law*. He has written several journal articles and chapters in books on issues related to constitutional law. He recently co-edited an edition of *Acta Juridica* titled *A Transformative Justice: Essays in Honour of Pius Langa* together with Alistair Price. In 2017, he was selected as one of South Africa's top 200 Young South Africans by the *Mail & Guardian*.

Jason Brickhill is a DPhil student in the Law Faculty. His research focuses on public interest litigation. He holds an LLB degree from the University of Cape Town and an MSt in international human rights law from the University of Oxford. After obtaining his law degree, Jason served as law clerk to Justice Kate O'Regan at the South African Constitutional Court. He has subsequently practised as an attorney (solicitor) and advocate (barrister) at the Johannesburg Bar and was previously the Director of the Constitutional Litigation Unit of the Legal Resources Centre, a South African public interest law firm. As an advocate, Jason appeared in the High Court, Supreme Court of Appeal and Constitutional Court of South Africa as well as the Supreme Court of Namibia. Jason is an editor of the *Constitutional Court Review*, a South African legal journal and an author of *Constitutional Litigation* (Juta, 2012) and has published widely in constitutional law and human rights law. He has taught constitutional law at the University of the Witwatersrand, Johannesburg and international human rights law at the University of Oxford.

Meghan Campbell is a Lecturer in Law at the University of Birmingham and Deputy-Director of the Oxford Human Rights Hub. Her research explores how the international human rights system can best respond to gender inequality and poverty. Her monograph *Women, Poverty, Equality* (Hart Publishing, 2018) explores how the concept of equality in the UN Convention on the Discrimination on the Elimination of All Forms of Discrimination Against Women can be interpreted to address gender-based poverty. She has published peer-reviewed articles on gender equality, human rights, the international legal system and public law and provided written evidence to the Joint Committee on Human Rights and Women and Equalities Committee on Brexit and human rights

Sandra Fredman is Rhodes Professor of the Laws of the British Commonwealth and the USA at the University of Oxford and Director of the Oxford Human Rights Hub. She was elected a Fellow of the British Academy in 2005 and became a QC (honoris causa) in 2012. She is Honorary Professor of Law at the University of Cape Town and a fellow of Pembroke College, Oxford. She has written and published widely on anti-discrimination law, human rights law and labour law, including numerous peer-reviewed articles, and three monographs: *Human Rights Transformed* (OUP, 2008); *Discrimination Law* (2nd ed, OUP, 2011); and *Women and the Law* (OUP, 1997), as well as two co-authored books: *The State as Employer* (Mansell, 1988) with Gillian Morris and *Labour Law and Industrial Relations in Great Britain* (2nd ed Kluwer, 1992) with Bob Hepple. She has also edited several books: *Discrimination and Human Rights: The Case of Racism* (OUP, 2001); and *Age as an Equality Issue* (Hart, 2003) with Sarah Spencer; and has written numerous articles in peer-reviewed law journals. She was awarded a three year Leverhulme Major Research Fellowship in 2004 to further her research into socio-economic rights and substantive equality. She is South African and holds degrees from the University of Witwatersrand and the University of Oxford. She has acted as an expert adviser on equality law and labour legislation in the EU, Northern Ireland, the UK, India, South Africa, Canada and the UN; and is a barrister practising at Old Square Chambers. She founded the Oxford Human Rights Hub in 2012, of which she is the Director.

Jayna Kothari is a co-founder of the Centre for Law and Policy Research. She practices as a Counsel in the Karnataka High Court and the Supreme Court of India. She graduated from University Law College with a B.A. LL.B degree and read the BCL at Oxford University. Jayna has been awarded the Wrangler D.C. Pavate Fellowship from Cambridge University. Jayna's research and practice interests include constitutional law, including the right to education, health and housing, gender, disability rights, environmental law. Her book, *The Future of Disability Law in India* was published in 2012 by Oxford University Press and is one of the first books on disability law in the country.

Gilbert Mitullah Omware is a PhD student at the Institute of Education, University College London. His research is focused on the comparative political economy dynamics of regulating low fee private schools in Kenya and Uganda. His research interests cover governance and regulation of education and the political economy of socioeconomic rights.

Conor O'Mahony is a senior lecturer at the School of Law at University College Cork, where he teaches and researches in the areas of constitutional law and children's rights. His research spans both areas independently, but particularly examines the constitutional rights of children, including a special focus on rights in educational settings. His book, *Educational Rights in Irish Law*, was published by Thomson Round Hall in 2006 and he has published numerous articles and book chapters considering the educational rights of children in the context of special educational needs, religious freedom and child protection in outlets including *Public Law*, the *Child and Family Law Quarterly* and the *Journal of Social Welfare and Family Law*. He is Deputy Director of the Child Law Clinic at UCC, through which academic staff and postgraduate students work to support litigation and advocate for law reform in the broad area of children's rights. One example of this work was the case of *O'Keeffe v Ireland* (2014) before the Grand Chamber of the European Court of Human Rights (on which his contribution to this collection is based), with which the Clinic was centrally involved.

Melanie Smuts trained as a human rights lawyer and has been passionate about new approaches to South African education since university where she was involved in and directed a number of education non-profits. In 2013, she founded Streetlight Schools – a non-profit pioneering innovative primary schools to address the achievement shortfall in primary education in South Africa through a focus on enquiry, collaboration, exploration, relevance and the use of technology to teach and learn.

Helen Taylor studied BA Honours (English Literature) and LLB at the University of Stellenbosch, South Africa, before coming to Oxford as a Rhodes Scholar. She completed the BCL with distinction at Balliol College and is currently reading for the DPhil in Law under the supervision of Prof. Sandra Fredman. Her research considers the design of remedies for enforcing the state's positive duties in human rights. Helen is a Research Director at the Oxford Human Rights Hub, working extensively on projects relating to the right to education. During her time at Oxford, she has been a member of the Oxford Pro Bono Publico executive committee and undertook an internship at UN Women in New York.

Yana van Leeve grew up in Cape Town where she studied a B.Soc. Sci in Industrial Sociology and Political Science at the University of Cape Town and an LLB at the University of the Western Cape, during which she was elected Chairperson of Students for Law and Social Justice (SLSJ). She began working for the Legal Resources Centre (LRC) in 2009, before joining Equal Education as the Deputy National Coordinator in 2013. In 2015, she was a law research clerk to Justice Edwin Cameron at the Constitutional Court of South Africa. Yana currently works as an attorney in an administrative law practice at a Johannesburg law firm and is a member of Equal Education's National Council.

Foreword

The realisation of the right of education is beset with enormous challenges today. Growing inequalities all over the world have their repercussions on the education system, resulting in increasing disparities in the accessibility and quality of education. The universality of the right to education is crippled by the exclusion and marginalisation that undermines educational opportunities for minorities, indigenous peoples, refugees, immigrants, the disabled, nomads, children from poor families, and other vulnerable sections of society. Girls are victims of discriminatory practices in education across many parts of the world, in spite of their equal right to education. Poverty, which is an affront to human dignity and a violation of human rights, is the biggest obstacle to realising the right to education. All those who are victims of poverty in the world today need education to break vicious cycles of disadvantage and disempowerment. The principles of social justice and equity which are at the core of the global mission of the United Nations to promote peace, development and human dignity, should guide our efforts to overcome these challenges in education.

All of these educational deprivations denote a lack of full compliance by states with their international obligations for the provision of free, basic education for all. Moreover, education as a public function of states is being eroded on account of unbridled privatisation. Private providers have been making inroads into education at all levels. The disparities in education have been exacerbated by privatisation owing to scant regulation by public authorities. Sprawling low-fee private schools operate in many developing countries, often showing disregard for the basic norms and principles of the right to education but seldom being held to account. Fast-growing private education institutions are also becoming predominant at the tertiary level. Funded and managed by individual proprietors or enterprises, privatisation is driven by business interests in education, or 'edu-business', which is detrimental to education as a public good. Governments, rather than acting against these trends, seem to be abdicating their responsibility to realise the right to education by disinvesting in education as a public good and, in some cases, even actively supporting privatisation.

These trends call for serious reflection as they erode the legal and moral foundations of the right to education as established by international human rights instruments. Access to private educational establishments owned by individual proprietors or enterprises is based upon the capacity to pay fees, which are often exorbitant, and implicates several prohibited grounds of discrimination in international human rights conventions. This qualified access breeds exclusion and social and cultural segregation. Moreover, corruption by private providers in education remains unaddressed due to the lack of adequate financial regulation and public scrutiny of their operations. A comprehensive and sound regulatory framework, which is prescriptive, prohibitive and punitive, is necessary for safeguarding the right to education from the risks posed by privatisation.

Privatisation may also have a nexus with arrangements to provide education through public–private partnerships. Such partnerships do not change the nature of the right to education or the state's obligations. The state remains both the guarantor and regulator on account of its obligations to respect, protect and promote the right to education. A differentiated approach in public–private partnerships is necessary so as to distinguish partners with private business interests in education from all those committed to the social cause of education, especially those with genuine philanthropic spirit. Emphasis should be placed on accountability, in the first place of governments, and, through them, of all non-state providers of education.

We must always bear in mind that the right to education is an inalienable right of every child – boys and girls alike. It is not a privilege of the rich and well-to-do, but rather a core obligation of all states and a moral imperative. It is incumbent upon governments, on account of their human rights obligations, to preserve education as a public good and expand opportunities for quality public education for all, free of charge. Greater advocacy for education as a universal right is of foremost importance to ensure that education is provided without discrimination or exclusion. States have international legal obligations to respect, protect and fulfil the right to education as laid down in these conventions. These obligations remain even where education is privatised.

In tandem with privatisation, there is also a trend towards the pursuit of materialistic values in education, whereby education is reduced to having an instrumental function, devoid of human rights values. This is detrimental to 'the full development of human personality' as an essential objective of education, enshrined in the Universal Declaration of Human Rights. The humanistic mission of education is being undermined rather than being fostered as the inspiration for education systems. Moreover, education should enable children and adults to develop attitudes and behaviour patterns that demonstrate solidarity and respect for cultural and religious diversity, provided this is in full conformity with the human rights values.

These considerations bear on the goal of improving the quality of education through greater empowerment in terms of knowledge, values, skills and competences that learners should attain. This goal cannot be reached without intensifying normative action at national level with respect to minimum quality standards. Quality and equity must remain uppermost in approaches to developing the education systems of tomorrow, recognising education as the foundation for human development and as being invaluable for individual and social transformation. A human rights approach, as embraced by the World Education Forum (Incheon, May 2015), provides this wider perspective by recognising the heavy responsibility of governments on account of their human rights obligations. A human rights perspective also enables us to understand and better appreciate that the right to education is not only as a human right in itself but it is also essential for the exercise of all other human rights. A human rights-based approach, with the right to education placed at centre stage, is a valuable policy tool for evaluating laws, policies and programmes in the field of education.

The right to education is not a matter of mere aspiration, but it is a legally enforceable entitlement. A citizen should have legal recourse in case of a breach, denial or violation of his or her right to education. The judiciary bears the onerous responsibility of safeguarding the right to education, as do other quasi-judicial national and international mechanisms, including the United Nations human rights treaty bodies, regional or national human rights commissions and ombudspersons. Independent complaints procedures and legal assistance to access the judicial system are valuable mechanisms for obtaining effective remedies to redress violations of the right to education. Public interest litigation also plays an important role in defending the right to education and holding the state and private providers to account for its enforcement.

It is heartening that these crucial challenges and related concerns are addressed through the central themes covered in this publication. This edited collection is particularly valuable for the way it pools together knowledge and expertise in an interdisciplinary spirit through scholarly contributions from a diverse range of educationalists, academics, human rights activists and sociologists from both developing and developed countries. Researchers, scholars, academics, human rights students and activists engaged in defending and promoting the right to education can all usefully draw upon the publication, and it serves as a source of reference for guiding public policy responses to challenges in realising the right to education.

The publication will be an especially valuable contribution to the global debate on the implementation of the 2030 Sustainable

Development Agenda adopted at the United Nations Summit in September 2015, which reaffirms the importance of the Universal Declaration of Human Rights as well as other international instruments relating to human rights and international law. Its human rights approach will no doubt impart strength to building inclusive and equitable education systems. This is all the more opportune in the context of the work of the High-Level Political Forum on the 2030 Agenda for Sustainable Development, with 'no one is left behind' as its leitmotiv, and in giving primacy to 'Upholding human rights and human dignity everywhere'. Education is of paramount importance in advancing in that direction and the centrality of education in all Sustainable Development Goals must therefore receive full recognition.

I have great pleasure in commending this publication devoted to the cause of education, of which both the individual and society are beneficiaries. With its focus on universality and the 'core' responsibility of states, I have no doubt that this publication will enrich reflections on how best to transform the right to education from an ideal into reality.

Kishore Singh
United Nations Special Rapporteur on the Right to Education
(August 2010 to July 2016)

Human rights and equality in education: Introduction

Sandra Fredman, Meghan Campbell and Helen Taylor

Education is at the heart of the global struggle to alleviate poverty and reduce inequality. It has been demonstrated that one extra year of education is associated with a reduction in inequality (as measured by the Gini coefficient) of 1.4 percentage points.[1] Yet it is precisely the most disadvantaged who face the greatest obstacles to accessing quality education. Although some progress has been made in recent decades, there were still as many as 57 million out-of-school children of primary school age in 2015.[2] Many of these will never access education. What role, then, can human rights play in addressing these issues? Education has been recognised as a fundamental human right at least since 1948, when the Universal Declaration of Human Rights declared that everyone has the right to free and compulsory education. Importantly, the right extends beyond access to education. It also includes quality education. Education must be 'directed to the full development of the human personality' and 'promote understanding, tolerance and friendship among all nations, racial or religious groups'.[3] The right to education has also been recognised in the major international human rights instruments, and in the domestic law of numerous countries.

This volume asks what role human rights can play in addressing some of the most challenging issues in the quest for quality education for all. We provide case studies from both the global South and the global North. The challenges are surprisingly similar, despite marked differences in development. From the South, we focus on India, Kenya and South Africa. Both countries face an enormous chasm between the ideal of equal rights to quality education and the reality; each has relatively recently given entrenched constitutional status to the right to education; and both have seen human rights litigation play an important part. From the global North, we look at New York State,

---

[1] Using data for 114 countries in the 1985–2005 period: 'Quality education: why it matters', www.un.org/sustainabledevelopment/wp-content/uploads/2017/02/ENGLISH_Why_it_Matters_Goal_4_QualityEducation.pdf.

[2] *The Millennium Development Goals Report 2015*, New York: United Nations.

[3] Universal Declaration of Human Rights, Article 26(2).

1

where educational disadvantage, in the midst of the richest country in the world, is even more striking. Although there is no constitutional right to education at federal level, the right is entrenched in the New York State constitution, and human rights litigation has been utilised in the quest for a better quality of education for disadvantaged inner-city children. Even where, as in Ireland, there is a long tradition of provision of education, the rights of children to safety and dignity within educational institutions have been at risk, and, here too, human rights litigation has yielded important principles applicable more generally. The book also deals with some of the ways in which these challenges can be addressed through international human rights law, both in relation to the right to education and the right to equality.

The first section of the book deals with the pressing issue of private provision of education, whether through faith schools, non-profit organisations or the mushrooming commercial sector of low-fee schools. The use of private providers is challenging for a human rights-based approach, which tends to the focus on the duties of the state. Can the state escape its responsibilities for fulfilling the right when schools are in private hands? Or can the state be held accountable for ensuring the right to quality education whether the provider is public or private? As Conor O'Mahony's chapter shows, this was in essence the question before the European Court of Human Rights (ECtHR) in *O'Keeffe v Ireland*.[4] In a landmark judgment, the Court held that the state had a positive obligation to take reasonable measures to prevent, detect and investigate rights violations by private parties in the provision of education to children. Although the case was concerned with the specific right to freedom from inhuman and degrading treatment in schools, O'Mahony argues that *O'Keeffe* provides a compelling framework for ensuring state accountability for all rights violations in private schools. Moreover, it applies to the non-profit and the profit sector alike, including, as in this case, the Catholic Church.

The situation in Kenya is more complex, as Gilbert Mitullah Omware's chapter shows. The author critically assesses the efforts of the Kenyan government to address the rise of private actors in education. Mitullah insightfully observes that private provision of education is not the result of happenstance but is the direct result of the shifts in international aid policies. The pressures from international organisations have resulted in a severe reduction of public services. Private actors, including foreign corporations, often supported by large donor organisations and developed countries, have filled this gap in

---

[4]   *O'Keeffe v Ireland*, 35810/09, 28 January 2014.

education targeting low-income families. The chapter reflects on the government's response and concludes it has been at best a patchwork approach, leaves low-income families vulnerable to exploitation and falls far short of human rights standards. Regulations remain unenforced and private schools often avoid registration, employ unqualified teachers and do not use the required curriculum. To guarantee a right to education for all learners, Mitullah proposes the concept of negotiated boundaries. All stakeholders involved in education must come to the table to develop a comprehensive regulatory framework based on human rights norms for private providers of education.

Melanie Smuts provides a much more positive perspective on the potential of private actors to provide good-quality education which is more flexible, more child-friendly and far less bureaucratic than state-provided education. Smuts focuses on the ways in which non-profit education, by being responsive to local community needs, can overcome legacies of racism, sexism and colonialism as well as pioneering pedagogical innovations. This demonstrates that, with good faith and energy, high-quality education can be provided. The difficulty for a human rights approach arises where the opposite outcomes occur, whether in the public or private sector. Brickhill and van Leeve, in their chapter, are sceptical and note that both for-profit and non-profit schools 'make compromises in critical areas'. To achieve the promise of equal education for all, human rights advocates need to confront the complicated challenges raised by the increasing numbers of private actors in the delivery of education.

Gilbert Mitullah Omware's chapter highlights a second theme running through the book as a whole, namely, how human rights law responds to attempts by those privileged in the education sector to retain that privilege. This theme is taken up in the chapter by Jayna Kothari. At one level, the Supreme Court of India has been robust, rejecting a challenge from private school proprietors arguing that the RTE Act (Right of Children to Free and Compulsory Education Act 2009) interfered with their freedom of occupation. However, the Court simultaneously provided an exemption for private unaided minority schools, on the basis that they were entitled to preserve their minority character. In a subsequent decision, the Court extended this exemption to minority schools even if they received state funding. The result of the two judgments is to exempt all minority schools from all the requirements of the RTE Act. Kothari's chapter shows how this has led to a large number of private schools falsely claiming minority status. More fundamentally, she concludes, there is no need for minority schools to be exempt from the norms and standards in the

RTE Act. Compliance would in no way violate any rights of minority instruction. But exempting such schools from these basic requirements 'seriously compromises the RTE Act's vision of providing equal access to quality education for all children'.

Michael Bishop's chapter faces a similar conundrum in a context in which minority rights risk protecting privileged minorities at the expense of poor and disadvantaged majorities. Although Afrikaans is a minority language in South Africa, it was the language of the dominant power under Apartheid, and Afrikaans-medium schools in democratic South Africa retain the privileges of the Apartheid era. Bishop shows how protection of Afrikaans as a medium of instruction excludes many poor black learners who could benefit from English-medium education. He therefore argues that it is not possible to apply the ordinary principles concerning minority languages to Afrikaans. At the same time, Afrikaners are entitled to some protection for their language. This requires 'compromises and innovative solutions that acknowledge both the position of privilege built on a history of racial discrimination, and the legitimate demand for protecting Afrikaans-language education'.

Rights of access to education are of little value if the quality of the education provided is poor. The unfortunate reality is that it is the most disadvantaged who are most at risk of receiving low-quality education. Helen Taylor's chapter therefore asks what a human rights approach can contribute to achieving both quality and equality in education. She brings these questions into focus by considering the long-running litigation in New York, where the applicants argued that the chronic underfunding of schools in inner-city New York breached their right to adequate education in the New York State constitution. The result of insufficient allocation of budget to these schools, which catered to predominantly African American and other poor ethnic minority children, was to create noticeable discrepancies between the quality of education they provided and the quality of schools serving a wealthier, largely white population. Her analysis of the litigation, brought by the Campaign for Fiscal Equity, demonstrates the value of a human rights-based assessment for achieving quality education for all. Importantly, the series of judgments in the case established a positive duty on the state to provide sufficient budget to provide adequate education, as well as setting out the principles by which adequacy should be assessed. Helen Taylor also analyses the complex interaction between the court and elected representatives in the state government, concluding that as long as a court is sensitive to the socio-political context, it is well placed to provide appropriate remedies to achieve quality education.

The obstacles to equality facing girls in education are particularly pronounced. Sandra Fredman argues in her chapter that in achieving gender equality, it is not sufficient to regard equality as merely entailing parity between girls and boys. Simply treating girls and boys in the same way will not address the gendered power relations which lead to ongoing inequality in education and beyond. Instead, it is argued that the principle of substantive equality should be the framework for evaluating progress towards equality in education. This requires attention to be paid to four mutually enhancing dimensions of equality: redressing disadvantage; addressing stigma, stereotyping, prejudice and violence; facilitating participation; and accommodating difference and achieving structural change. This is particularly relevant in the light of the Sustainable Development Goals, which have committed the world both to ensuring inclusive and equitable quality education and to achieve gender equality and empower all women and girls by 2030.

Meghan Campbell's chapter focuses in detail on one crucial requirement in the search of equality for women, namely sex education. She argues that the delivery of human rights-based sex education is a positive obligation on the state to fulfil girl's right to equal education and gender equality under the Convention on the Elimination of Discrimination Against Women (CEDAW). Campbell demonstrates how the lack of good-quality sex education can have a devastating effect on the lives of girls and women. This raises the complex problem of how to mediate potential obstacles raised by conservative religious and cultural norms, echoing the difficulty of reconciling minority rights with access to education for all. Campbell argues that a human rights approach offers a framework to reconcile these rights, particularly through the requirement that any limitation on rights should be justified as a necessary and proportionate. She concludes that 'due to the significance of the human rights that are fulfilled by sex education, it is necessary and proportionate to limit the role of conservative religious and cultural norms in delivery of sex education in the classroom'.

Brickhill and van Leeve's chapter revisits the contestation between those wishing to retain their privileged access to educational resources and those who are shut out of those resources. The South African constitution differs from international human rights law, in that it does not provide for a right to free education. Although the poorest quintiles are entitled to free education, public schools in more affluent areas are fee paying. Most of the latter are schools which were established in the Apartheid era to cater for white students, and which received generous state funding, as compared to the derisory subsidies paid to schools catering for black children under Apartheid. The resulting two-tier public school system has effectively been maintained, mainly because school fees payable to the schools in affluent areas are largely retained by the school, in addition to public subsidies. In stark contrast, schools in disadvantaged areas are woefully underfunded. Indeed, in rural areas such as the Eastern Cape, many learners are still educated in classrooms made of mud, with no furniture, a deficit of teachers and no textbooks. Brickhill and van Leeve document how these polar opposites have led to two parallel streams of litigation under the right to education. As they put it: 'On the one hand, we see claims to maintain control of existing public resources at better-off schools; and, on the other, increasing pressure for provision of the education inputs that are already available at the wealthier, well-stocked schools.' They conclude, as do several of the authors in this volume, that a human rights framework is capable of mediating these conflicts. In the first stream of cases, the South African Constitutional Court was clear that the focus of all role players should be on the rights of students; while in the cases dealing with infrastructure and resources, courts have created a vision of education as an empowerment right. Human rights litigation, rather than being seen as providing definitive answers, should be regarded as functioning as an arena within which different groups can engage and collaborate in giving substance to the right to quality education.

Conclusion

Sceptics have questioned whether human rights offer any added value to the struggle for high-quality education for all learners. The chapters in this collection are a powerful rebuttal of these claims and demonstrate the manifold ways in which human rights enrich discussions on education. Access to high-quality education is becoming increasingly complicated. There are competing agendas on the delivery of education and, as a result, insufficient attention is paid to how education can reinforce hierarchies and disadvantage. Human rights can go to the heart of current challenges. Its unshakeable commitment to non-discrimination and equality shines the spotlight on the most disadvantaged learners. Human rights provides a framework for evaluating tensions between different actors in education – majority versus minority interests, public versus private actors – without losing sight of the primary importance of realising education for all, including children belonging to religious, linguistic, racial or ethnic minorities and children belonging to other marginalised sections of society, such as girls or rural children. At the same time, human rights opens up accountability forums at the domestic and international level so that disadvantaged learners can claim their rights to access high-quality education and participate as equals in developing education laws, policies and programmes. The promise of achieving inclusive and lifelong learning for all people can only be achieved when we recognise the central importance of human rights in education.

Part I
The role of public and private actors in education

Public rights and private schools: state accountability for violations of rights in education

Conor O'Mahony

Introduction

When we think of education and the human rights obligations of the state, we most often think of children having a right to education. This right is widely recognised in international law, as is the corresponding obligation on the state to vindicate it.[1] Moreover, the right to education is the most commonly recognised right of children in national constitutions.[2] Less attention tends to be paid to children's rights in education,[3] such as the right to participate in decisions affecting them, the right to protection from harm, the right to dignified punishment and the right to religious freedom. While these rights are well recognised in international human rights law (most particularly the UN Convention on the Rights of the Child 1989 [CRC] and the European Convention on Human Rights 1950 [ECHR]), they are often not the subject of specific domestic law provisions setting out clear state responsibility for vindicating these rights in an educational setting.

Securing state accountability for vindicating the rights of children in education becomes particularly challenging in the context of

---

[1] See generally D. Hodgson, *The human right to education*, Aldershot: Ashgate, 1998.

[2] C. Grabenwarter, J. Helgesen, A. Peters, H. Thorgeirsdottir, A. Lindboe, U. Kilkelly and C. O'Mahony, *The protection of children's rights: International standards and domestic constitutions*, Strasbourg: Council of Europe, 2014, www.venice.coe. int/webforms/documents/?pdf=CDL-AD(2014)005-e, p 17.

[3] C. Hamilton, 'Rights of the child: a right to education and a right in education', in M. Davey and C. Bridge (eds), *Family law toward the millennium*, London: Butterworths, 1997, p 203: 'A child's right to an education is not just the right to receive some form of schooling. Children's rights in education are wider than this and can be most neatly summed up as rights to education, rights in education and rights *through* education' (emphasis in original).

private schools (whether fully private or some form of public–private partnership). In these schools, a private organisation is interposed between the rights-holder (the child) and the duty-bearer (the state). This poses the question of where responsibility lies if a child's rights are not vindicated. Can the state avoid being held accountable for a rights violation on the basis that a private actor is responsible for the act or omission involved – or does the state bear residual responsibility for ensuring that the rights of children in education are vindicated, regardless of the status of the school that they attend?

In essence, this was the question that confronted the European Court of Human Rights (ECtHR) in *O'Keeffe v Ireland*.[4] While that case was focused on a violation of one specific right – namely, the right to freedom from inhuman and degrading treatment – its significance is much broader, and its central finding could, in principle, apply to any right held by children within the education system. The Grand Chamber's framing of the issue in terms of positive obligations and the taking of reasonable measures to prevent, detect and investigate rights violations provides a compelling framework for ensuring state accountability for rights violations in private schools. This chapter will briefly outline the factual background to the case and the reasoning of the Court, before concluding by assessing its broader implications outside of the immediate context of the sexual abuse of children.

Background: the Irish primary school system

Ireland is unusual in the way in which its primary school system, in spite of the use of the term 'National School', is not at all national or public – it is, in fact, a system of private schools, overwhelmingly owned and managed by religious denominations, with the small remainder owned and managed by organisations committed to the provision of a multi-denominational alternative. The roots of this system are historical and pre-date the 1937 Constitution of Ireland quite considerably; indeed, they can be traced to the very beginning of the system of state-funded education in Ireland in 1833.[5] When Eamonn de Valera, the architect of the Irish Constitution of 1937, came to draft its educational provisions, one of his greatest concerns was the maintenance of the status quo – so much so that when de Valera was presented with a draft of Article 42.4

[4] *O'Keeffe v Ireland*, 35810/09, 28 January 2014.
[5] See further C. O'Mahony, 'Religious education in Ireland', in D. Davis and E. Miroshnikova (eds), *Routledge international handbook of religious education*, Oxford: Routledge, 2013, pp 156–8.

that referred to a duty on the state to 'provide free primary education', he altered this to 'provide for' in his own handwriting.[6] Gerard Quinn has observed: 'The main intention of Article 42 seems to have been to copperfasten [the] historic arrangement between Church and State. It had less to do with the substantive right to education of the child and more to do with protecting the arrangement between the funders of education (the State), the providers of education (the religious bodies) and the parents.'[7]

In *Crowley v Ireland*, Kenny J in the Supreme Court confirmed that the use of the phrase 'provide for' in Article 42.4 keeps the state at one remove from the actual provision of education:

> The effect of this is that the State is to provide the buildings, to pay the teachers who are under no contractual duty to it but to the manager or trustees, to provide means of transport to the school if this is necessary to avoid hardship, and to prescribe minimum standards.[8]

During the middle part of the 20th century, the Irish education system experienced a widespread and appalling incidence of both physical and sexual abuse perpetrated on children by various authority figures, including teachers, priests, nuns and other school staff. By its nature, such abuse was more prevalent at residential institutions, where children were permanently under the authority of the staff and did not go home at the end of a school day, but a not insignificant amount of abuse also took place at non-residential educational institutions. Most significantly, and related to the outsourcing of education provision to religious organisations, a culture of inadequate state supervision and child protection was endemic in the education system as a whole, with the result that wherever abuse did occur, it went unchecked over lengthy periods of time.

[6] M. Farry, *Education and the constitution*, Dublin: Round Hall, Sweet & Maxwell, 1996, p 13; *Report of the Constitution Review Group*, Dublin: Stationery Office, 1996, p 344.

[7] G. Quinn, 'Rethinking the nature of economic, social and cultural rights in the Irish legal order', in C. Costello (ed.), *Fundamental social rights: Current European legal protection and the challenge of the EU Charter on Fundamental Rights*, Dublin: Irish Centre for European Law, 2000, p 49. See further D. Clarke, 'Education, the state and sectarian schools', in T. Murphy and P. Twomey (eds), *Ireland's evolving constitution*, Oxford: Hart Publishing, 1998, pp 66–7.

[8] [1980] IR 102 at 126.

The Commission to Inquire into Child Abuse Act 2000 established a commission chaired by Mr Justice Seán Ryan, which published its final report ('the Ryan Report') on 20 May 2009.[9] The Ryan Report documented a 'consistently high level of sexual crime against young boys and girls' in Ireland in the middle part of the 20th century.[10] It found that sexual abuse was endemic in boys' institutions and also occurred in many girls' institutions; that the system of inspection carried out by the Department of Education was flawed and incapable of being effective, and that the Department's deferential and submissive attitude towards the religious congregations compromised its ability to carry out inspection and monitoring of schools. Cases of sexual abuse were managed with a view to minimising the risk of public disclosure and damage to the institution and religious order involved; members of religious orders accused of abuse were not reported to the Gardaí (Irish police); religious authorities responded to evidence of sexual abuse by transferring the offender to another location where, in many instances, he was free to offend again; and perpetrators of abuse were able to operate undetected for long periods at the core of institutions. The clear conclusion that can be drawn from the findings of the Ryan Report is that, in addition to the fault and blame that attaches to individual perpetrators of abuse, an enormous degree of fault can be attributed to a systemic failure to prevent and detect sexual abuse in the Irish education system.[11]

The Louise O'Keeffe case: national litigation

This was the system and the context in which Louise O'Keeffe received her primary education. She attended Dunderrow National School, a Catholic denominational school which was owned by the Bishop of Cork and Ross and managed by the local Catholic parish priest. Over the first six months of 1973, she was the victim of a series of sexual assaults by the school principal. A complaint had first been made to the school manager regarding sexual abuse by this teacher two years earlier in 1971; this complaint was not reported to the police, to the Department of Education or to any other state authority and was not acted upon by the manager. Some months after Louise O'Keeffe was abused, other parents complained to the school regarding allegations

---

[9] S. Ryan, *Commission to Inquire into Child Abuse Report*, Dublin: Stationery Office, 2009, available at www.childabusecommission.com.

[10] Ryan, *Commission to Inquire into Child Abuse Report*, p 21.

[11] Ryan, *Commission to Inquire into Child Abuse Report*, at pp 451–9.

of sexual abuse made by their children against the principal. In light of these allegations, having initially gone on sick leave, the teacher later resigned his post and moved to another school, where he taught for another 22 years without any further allegations being made against him. The Department of Education was not informed of the allegations, although it was notified of the change of personnel.

After the principal had retired from teaching in 1995, complaints were made to the Gardaí in 1996 regarding abuse alleged to have taken place at Dunderrow. During the course of the investigations, Louise O'Keeffe made a statement to the Gardaí regarding her case. The principal pleaded guilty in 1998 to 21 sample charges out of a total of 386 relating to sexual abuse of girls under his care at Dunderrow, and was sentenced to three years in prison. Louise O'Keeffe was awarded IR£53,000 by the Criminal Injuries Compensation Tribunal. The process of making a statement against her abuser, and his subsequent conviction, had a profound impact on her. She came to realise that what had happened to her as a child was far more significant and important than she had previously thought, and was closely connected to other difficulties she had experienced in her life, including those which led to the breakdown of her marriage.

Accordingly, with the aim of raising awareness of what had happened to her and to other girls, and who was responsible, Louise O'Keeffe instituted civil assault proceedings against the principal in 1998, and obtained judgment against him in default of appearance in 1999. However, Louise O'Keeffe's claim was not directed solely against the principal: she also instituted proceedings against the state. While her action contained more than one ground, the primary focus was vicarious liability of the state for the torts committed by the principal in the course of his employment.[12]

Both the High Court[13] and the Supreme Court[14] rejected the claim that the state bore vicarious liability for the school principal's actions. Primarily, the decision turned on the fact that although the principal's salary was paid by the state, he was, at all times, an employee of a privately owned school and not of the state. Accordingly, as the school was managed by the parish priest and not the state, the traditional rationale for vicarious liability (namely, that the employer exercises

---

[12] For an overview of the relevant principles of Irish law relating to vicarious liability, see B. McMahon and W. Binchy, *Law of torts*, 3rd edn, Haywards Heath: Tottel, 2000, ch 43.

[13] *LO'K v LH* [2006] IEHC 13.

[14] *O'Keeffe v Hickey* [2009] 2 IR 302.

control over the employee and should be liable for torts committed by employees under his control) did not apply.

From the perspective of accountability, the decisions of the domestic courts were extremely disappointing.[15] Their effect was to suggest that the state had no legal obligation whatsoever to implement child protection mechanisms in the education system and that the protection of children from harm in school was a task left entirely in the domain of school management. In essence, the state was allowed to hide behind the historical structure of outsourcing its duty to educate so as to abdicate any responsibility for protecting the rights of children in education, or any accountability for breaches of those rights that could be attributed to state actions or inactions.

The issue of state inaction was particularly relevant in the context of the *O'Keeffe* case. If it is accepted that the school principal was not a state employee, then it is clear that the state did not abuse Louise O'Keeffe. However, it is equally clear that the state did little or nothing to protect her from being abused. There was no child protection framework in place in Irish schools in the 1970s; the state seems to have viewed this as a matter for individual schools and school patrons rather than a matter in respect of which the state bore any duty or responsibility. The consequences of this approach were described by Fennelly J:

> The calamity of the exploitation of authority over children so to abuse them sexually has shaken society to its foundations. Cases of sexual abuse have preoccupied our criminal courts and this Court for many years. It is surprising that here for the first time this Court is confronted with questions relating to the liability of institutions, extending to the State itself, for sexual abuse perpetrated, as in this case, on schoolchildren in a national school, by a teacher.[16]

Similarly, Geoghegan J, in his dissenting judgment, commented that '[r]egrettably, this court has become aware through the numerous judicial review cases seeking to stop criminal trials that in many instances there have been alleged sexual assaults by teachers in a semi-concealed

---

15 For a detailed critique, see C. O'Mahony, 'State liability for abuse in primary schools: systemic failure and *O'Keeffe v. Hickey*', *Irish Educational Studies*, 28(3) (2009): 315–31.

16 *O'Keeffe v Hickey* [2009] 2 IR 302 at 361.

fashion in the actual classroom while teaching'.[17] Indeed, the Supreme Court later declined to award costs to the state against Louise O'Keeffe on the basis that her case concerned a complex point of law affecting 'a substantive volume of [sex abuse] cases … a significant number of which involve teachers whose salary is paid by the State', and that 'their number reflects the fact that they are the accumulation of claims of wrongdoing extending over the past three or four decades'.[18] In this light, there can be little doubt that incidents of sexual abuse in the Irish education system were far from unusual and isolated incidents; on the contrary, they were an entirely foreseeable and relatively widespread consequence of the absence of effective measures being implemented by the state to prevent and detect such abuse. More particularly, the abuse suffered by Louise O'Keeffe was not an isolated or unforeseeable incident in her particular school; in the criminal proceedings, her abuser pleaded guilty to 21 sample charges out of 386 in total, and Louise O'Keeffe was one of the later victims. Nevertheless, the narrow tort law focus of the domestic litigation left a situation where a child's rights in education had clearly been violated, but the state could not be held to account for its failure to take any steps to ensure those rights would be protected against an all-too-obvious threat.

The Louise O'Keeffe case: Strasbourg litigation

That every child has the right to be protected from sexual abuse in school and that the state had failed in its duty to protect Louise O'Keeffe from such abuse was the central argument in the case of *O'Keeffe v Ireland* before the ECtHR. While at national level, the argument had focused on whether the state could be held vicariously liable for the actions of a teacher, in Strasbourg the argument focused on direct liability for the state's inaction in failing to implement a child protection framework in primary schools. This subtle but significant shift of focus sought to engage the state's positive obligations under the ECHR.

The case hinged on the argument that no effective measures were in place to detect and prevent child abuse in primary schools. Had such measures been in place, the school principal would have been removed from his position far earlier and his litany of abuse would never have been allowed to go as far as it did. This argument relied first on Article 3 of the ECHR, which prohibits torture and inhuman and degrading treatment and punishment, read together with Article 1,

[17] *O'Keeffe v Hickey* [2009] 2 IR 302 at 346–7.
[18] *O'Keeffe v Hickey* [2009] IESC. 39.

which requires that states secure to everyone within their jurisdiction the rights and freedoms defined in the Convention. Second, it relied on Article 13 of the Convention, which provides that '[e]veryone whose rights and freedoms as set forth in [the] Convention are violated shall have an effective remedy before a national authority'. Louise O'Keeffe argued that Articles 1 and 3 of the ECHR gave her a right to be protected from sexual abuse, and placed a duty on the state to provide such protection; her Article 3 right was violated by the failure of the Irish state to implement effective child protection measures in primary schools in the 1970s, and her Article 13 right was violated by her inability to secure a remedy in domestic law for this failure.

Underpinning her argument were the earlier cases of *A v United Kingdom*[19] and *Z v United Kingdom*.[20] In each of these cases, the United Kingdom had been found to have violated Convention rights by failing to implement effective measures to protect children from physical violence and sexual abuse in the family home. In *Z*, the Court stated that Article 3, read together with Article 1 of the Convention, imposes a positive duty on states to take measures designed to ensure that individuals within their jurisdiction are not subjected to torture or inhuman or degrading treatment, including such ill-treatment administered by private individuals. These measures should provide effective protection, in particular, for children and other vulnerable persons, and include reasonable steps to prevent ill-treatment of which the authorities had or ought to have had knowledge.[21]

Louise O'Keeffe's argument was that if the state had a positive obligation to protect children in the family home, it similarly had an obligation to protect children in school, whether that school was public or private. The Irish authorities 'ought' to have had knowledge that children in primary schools were at risk of (and were frequently victims of) sexual abuse, and accordingly were obliged to implement measures designed to protect children against such abuse. While Hardiman J had stated in the Supreme Court that 'the Minister can hardly be responsible for a failure to "cease" a course of action of whose existence he was quite unaware',[22] the argument presented in Strasbourg was that, pursuant to the duties identified in *A v United Kingdom* and *Z v United Kingdom*, the minister should have established and operated a

---

[19] (1999) 27 EHRR 611.
[20] (2002) 34 EHRR 97; see U. Kilkelly, *Children's rights in Ireland: Law, policy and practice*, Haywards Heath: Tottel, 2008, sections 8.013 to 8.014.
[21] (2002) 34 EHRR 97 at paras. 69–75.
[22] *O'Keeffe v Hickey* [2009] 2 IR 302 at 344.

system that ensured that he *was* aware that complaints of sexual abuse had been made against a school principal who committed nearly 400 acts in total. The prosecution of the perpetrator some twenty years after the event did not discharge the state's obligations in this regard.

In its judgment of 29 January 2014,[23] the Grand Chamber accepted all of these arguments. It found that under Article 3, it was an 'inherent positive obligation of government in the 1970s to protect children from ill-treatment', and that this obligation was 'of acute importance in a primary education context'.[24] It rejected the state's argument that it was not aware of the risk of abuse in Irish primary schools, since such crimes were (as documented in the Ryan Report) being prosecuted 'at a significant rate' at the time.[25] The state failed to fulfil its obligation when it entrusted the management of the primary education of the vast majority of young Irish children to denominational schools, without putting in place any mechanism of effective state control against the risks of abuse occurring.[26] Complaints were directed away from state authorities towards the school managers (usually parish priests), and school inspectors had no obligation to inquire into or monitor teachers' treatment of children.[27] Ultimately, the decision came down to a statement of the obvious by the Court: in a case where a single teacher committed almost 400 counts of sexual abuse on over 20 victims without being detected by the state, the child protection system simply had to be considered ineffective:

> Any system of detection and reporting which allowed such extensive and serious ill-conduct to continue for so long must be considered to be ineffective … Adequate action taken on the 1971 complaint could reasonably have been expected to avoid the present applicant being abused two years later by the same teacher in the same school.[28]

---

[23] *O'Keeffe v Ireland*, 35810/09, 28 January 2014. For a detailed commentary, see C. O'Mahony and U. Kilkelly, '*O'Keeffe v Ireland* and the duty of the state to identify and prevent child abuse', *Journal of Social Welfare and Family Law*, 36(3) (2014): 320–9 and J. Gallen, '*O'Keeffe v Ireland*: the liability of states for failure to provide an effective system for the detection and prevention of child sexual abuse in education', *Modern Law Review*, 78(1) (2015): 140–63.

[24] *O'Keeffe v Ireland*, 35810/09, 28 January 2014, para. 168.

[25] *O'Keeffe v Ireland*, 35810/09, 28 January 2014, para. 168.

[26] *O'Keeffe v Ireland*, 35810/09, 28 January 2014, para. 168.

[27] *O'Keeffe v Ireland*, 35810/09, 28 January 2014, para. 168.

[28] *O'Keeffe v Ireland*, 35810/09, 28 January 2014, at para. 166.

In addition to the violation of the right to freedom from inhuman and degrading treatment under Article 3, the Court also found that there was a violation of the right to an effective remedy under Article 13. Louise O'Keeffe had been able to establish before the courts her abuser's civil and criminal culpability, but the state was also culpable, and Irish law did not offer her an avenue to establish this culpability and to access an effective remedy for it.[29]

In their joint partly dissenting opinions, Judges Zupančić, Gyulumyan, Kalaydjieva, De Gaetano and Wojtyczek expressed their view that the reasoning of the majority was founded on an implicit assumption that educational systems with a strong state role or state participation offer better protection to children, which unnecessarily called into question the Irish model of education, which is deeply rooted in the nation's history.[30] It is difficult to find any support for this proposition in the majority judgment. The effect of the judgment is that the state's duty under Article 3 to take steps to detect and prevent child abuse applies equally in either state or private schools. The finding was not that the violation resulted from the reliance on private schools to discharge the state's obligation to educate; it resulted from the failure to implement an adequate child protection framework in such schools.[31] Precisely the same finding could be made in respect of an inadequate child protection framework in state schools.

While the decision in *O'Keeffe* was made in the context of sexual abuse and the right to freedom from inhuman and degrading treatment, there is no reason in principle why the same approach could not be applied to other rights. Viewed through the lens of the ECHR, the well-developed doctrine of positive obligations[32] can be brought to bear on any right by reading the relevant article in conjunction with Article 1, thus imposing an obligation on the state to take positive steps to prevent the rights of children being violated by school staff (or indeed by other children) within the confines of public or private schools.[33] To similar effect, any given provision of the Convention must

---

29   *O'Keeffe v Ireland*, 35810/09, 28 January 2014, paras. 183–7.
30   *O'Keeffe v Ireland*, 35810/09, 28 January 2014, Joint Partly Dissenting Opinions of Judges Zupančić, Gyulumyan, Kalaydjieva, De Gaetano and Wojtyczek, para. 19.
31   *O'Keeffe v Ireland*, 35810/09, 28 January 2014, para. 168.
32   See, e.g., U. Kilkelly, 'Protecting children's rights under the ECHR: the role of positive obligations', *Northern Ireland Legal Quarterly*, 61(3) (2010): 245–61.
33   In this regard, note that the Court referred broadly to a duty to protect children from rights violations 'administered by private individuals'; *O'Keeffe v Ireland*, 35810/09, 28 January 2014, para. 144.

be read in conjunction with the non-discrimination clause of Article 14. Where a child in school either suffers a substantive violation of a right in education, or is denied the equal protection of his or her rights in education, member states are obliged to provide an effective remedy in domestic law or they will fall foul of Article 13. To take one very plausible example: if a child was denied the free practice of religion, or subjected to religious discrimination, in a private school and it turned out that there was no domestic law framework providing a remedy for this, the principles established in *O'Keeffe* provide a pathway to arguing that this constitutes a violation of Article 9 (read in conjunction with either Articles 1 or Article 14) and Article 13. Article 3 could potentially be violated by a range of less serious conduct than the sexual abuse seen in O'Keeffe; a failure to prevent serious bullying by other pupils is one possible example.[34] Whatever the conduct, the key point, as stated by the Court in *Costello-Roberts v United Kingdom*, is that 'the State cannot absolve itself from responsibility by delegating its obligations to private bodies or individuals'.[35]

While this analysis is very focused on the ECHR system, the relevance and significance of the decision does not end there. The positive obligations mode of analysis has the potential to be applied in other spheres as well, most particularly in the interpretation of the CRC. The CRC contains detailed provisions setting out the rights of children – indeed, it is far more detailed than the ECHR in this regard – and many of these rights are highly applicable in an educational setting. The approach taken by the ECtHR in *O'Keeffe* could be used to frame arguments based on CRC provisions at an international level in complaints taken to the Committee on the Rights of the Child under Optional Protocol No. 3 to the CRC. In national courts, the same approach could also be utilised, particularly in jurisdictions where the CRC has been incorporated into domestic law; but also elsewhere, since it is not unknown for the CRC to be relied upon in judgments of courts even in jurisdictions where the CRC has not

---

[34] See, for example, *Dordevic v Croatia*, 41526/10, 24 July 2012.

[35] *Costello-Roberts v United Kingdom*, 13134/87, 25 March 1993, para. 27. A similar question was considered through the lens of negative obligations in the case of *Christian Education South Africa v Minister of Education* (CCT4/00) [2000] ZACC 11, in which the South African Constitutional Court rejected the argument that a law banning corporal punishment in all schools (including private religious schools) violated the right to religious freedom.

been incorporated.[36] Indeed, even the United States Supreme Court has referenced the CRC, notwithstanding the fact that the United States has yet to ratify the Convention.[37]

Finally, leaving aside international human rights law altogether, the principle that the state bears a positive obligation to protect the rights of children in education in private as well as public schools could be brought to bear in litigation based on domestic human rights law provisions (such as national constitutions, many of which include enforceable rights that apply to children in education). While the precise approach taken by the ECtHR may run into separation of powers difficulties in some jurisdictions, there may be significant scope in others for using domestic constitutional law to hold states accountable for failures to ensure that the constitutional rights of children are adequately protected within a private school setting.[38]

Conclusion

The central issue in the *O'Keeffe* case was accountability: who should be held culpable for the failure to protect a child's rights in education in a state-funded but privately owned and managed school? It is legitimate to argue that the state could not have eyes and ears in every classroom and that a duty to ensure that every child is protected from all rights violations would be impossible to execute – but the standard set down in *O'Keeffe* sets the bar much, much lower. The ECHR test is whether the state took reasonable steps to prevent rights violations, the risk of which the authorities had or ought to have had knowledge. Where the state fails in these obligations, the ECtHR has made it clear that victims should, as part of an effective remedy, be entitled to establish the liability of the state for any contributing acts or omissions, and to be awarded compensation accordingly. Allowing victims of rights violations to recover against the state on this basis provides them with

---

[36] For examples of judgments of national courts which rely on provisions of the CRC, see Children's Rights Information Network, *CRC in court: The case law of the Convention on the Rights of the Child*, available at www.crin.org/en/docs/CRC_in_Court_Report.pdf.

[37] See *Roper v Simmons*, 543 US 551 at 576 (2005). For a critique of this approach in the United States, see the dissenting judgment of Justice Scalia, *Roper v Simmons*, 543 US 551 at 622.

[38] For an example of what such an argument might look like, see C. O'Mahony, 'State liability for abuse in primary schools: systemic failure and *O'Keeffe v. Hickey*', *Irish Educational Studies*, 28(3) (2009): 321–31 at 315.

an effective remedy, and could act as a strong incentive for states to take effective measures to ensure that such cases do not arise in the future.

The alternative view, implicitly accepted by the Irish Supreme Court in *O'Keeffe v Hickey*, is that the state has no legal obligation whatsoever to take steps to protect the rights of children in private schools; and, as the Irish experience (exemplified by the *O'Keeffe* case and the Ryan Report) has shown, such a view has potentially disastrous consequences for the human rights of children. Against this backdrop, the key message of the *O'Keeffe* decision is a crucial one. Children have human rights while they are in school; they do not leave their rights behind at the school gate. The state has a direct obligation to protect the rights of children in all schools, whether fully public, fully private or something in between.

TWO

The dynamics of regulating low-fee private schools in Kenya

Gilbert Mitullah Omware

Introduction

The role of the government in the discourse on education has been transformed in many African countries with the increased participation of the private sector in education, whether through government initiatives or the efforts of the private sector.[1] This change, signalled by the gravitation towards neoliberal marketisation, marks the conversion of education from a contested space of knowledge to a more commodity-oriented space, where rules of the market influence change, growth and development. Education then teeters on the divide between a public and a private good.[2]

The Kenyan Constitution specifically protects a right to education. Articles 43(1)(f) and 53 of the Constitution of Kenya 2010 guarantee the right to education and children's right to basic education respectively. Despite numerous laws, regulations and policies implementing the right to education, there remains the reality of government failure to provide access to quality learning.[3] There is still a disconnection between the regulatory aspirations that facilitate the right to education and the actual implementation of programmes that realise this right. This has led to the mushrooming of numerous small, independent

---

[1]   Stephen J. Ball and Deborah Youdell, 'Hidden privatisation in public education', *Education Review*, 21 (2009): 73–83. James Tooley and Pauline Dixon, '"*De facto*" privatisation of education and the poor: implications of a study from sub-Saharan Africa and India', *Compare: A Journal of Comparative and International Education*, 36 (2006): 443–62.

[2]   Maria Balarin, 'The changing governance of education: a comparative political economy perspective on hybridity', *American Behavioral Sciences*, 58 (2014): 1446–63.

[3]   James Tooley, Pauline Dixon, Yarim Shamsan and Ian Schagen, 'The relative quality and cost-effectiveness of private and public schools for low-income families: a case study in a developing country', *School Effectiveness and School Improvement*, 21 (2010): 117–44.

low-fee private schools and the consequent introduction of larger, more corporate low-fee private school chains. The presence of these schools has elicited various government responses through policy and regulation.

Before considering these government responses, it is necessary to address the matter of varying terminology used across academia and education practice to refer to these kinds of private schools. The global discourse on private schools for the poor has yielded the terms 'low-cost' private schools and 'low-fee' private schools. I reject the use of the term 'low-cost' because, while the argument has been made that these schools charge relatively low user fees, the cost of attending them – both in financial and non-financial terms – is unclear, particularly when viewed through an equality, equity and social justice lens. In Kenya, the contextual term for 'low-fee' private schools is 'APBET' schools (Alternative Provision of Basic Education and Training), after the 2009 APBET Policy. Other terms that have been used in Kenya are 'complementary' schools and 'non-formal' schools. In this chapter, I will use 'low-fee' private schools and 'APBET' schools interchangeably, with the latter term used when highlighting issues relevant to the Kenyan context. Three categories of low-fee private schools can be identified using size and profit as distinguishing features. The first category captures small, non-profit low-fee private schools mostly run by non-governmental organisations (NGOs) or faith- and community-based organisations. The second covers small, for-profit low-fee private schools mostly run by individuals and self-help groups. The third is large, for-profit chains that are corporate, well resourced and operate on a large scale. These three kinds of schools all bear the same features in terms of infrastructure and operational model, and they maintain relatively similar quality standards.

This chapter raises the question of whether private provision can compensate for the state's failure to provide quality education. It explores Kenya's current approach to the regulation of low-fee private schools amid the tension between conceiving of education as a commodity provided for profit, where rules of the market determine growth and development, and conceiving of education as a fundamental right that the state must fulfil for every person in its jurisdiction. What role does a human rights approach have in ensuring that the provision of education, whether public or private, truly fulfils each individual child's right to education? The chapter examines these issues in the Kenyan context. It begins by explaining the social context which has led to the proliferation of low-fee private schools in Kenya. It then turns to consider the main regulatory vehicles that have been tried in Kenya. After a careful assessment of the regulation regimes, it concludes that the Kenyan approach to the regulation of low-fee private schools is at best a patchwork of ideas and approaches that has fallen far short of the standards required by human rights and the national aims of social justice and equality. This puts into question the future role of private schools in the provision of education, and accordingly raises the question of whether too little emphasis is currently placed on developing a robust public education sector. This argument is controversial as there is an inexorable pull towards private schools for parents desperate to ensure a high-quality education for their children. The analysis in this chapter shows the pivotal role of the state in the provision of education, with or without privatisation, and therefore the importance of a clearly structured and consistent approach to regulating education. The chapter concludes by proposing a framework for stakeholders to use when crafting, operationalising, and enforcing government education policy.

Growth and expansion of low-fee private schools in Kenya

The narrative on the growth of APBET schools in Kenya must be placed in the context of the global multi-pronged stakeholder participation that elicited their existence and expansion. Some developing countries gaining independence from colonial powers in the 1960s established education as a key pillar for nation-building and economic growth.[4] They worked towards ensuring there was free basic education, in line with the Universal Declaration of Human Rights and the attendant treaties that cemented a right to education.[5] At the same time, there was a push for economic empowerment through education in line with the human capital approach.

With the slowing down of economic growth in the 1980s, the World Bank and International Monetary Fund (IMF) enforced structural adjustment programs in developing countries, including

---

[4] Wanyama Pius Muricho and John Changách Koskey, 'Education reforms in Kenya for innovation', *International Journal of Humanities and Social Science*, 3 (2013): 123–45.

[5] UNICEF, *Abolishing school fees in Africa: Lessons from Ethiopia, Ghana, Kenya, Malawi, and Mozambique*, Washington DC, 2009, http://dx.doi.org/10.1596/978-0-8213-7540-2.

Kenya,[6] requiring public spending cuts on essential social services. In some developing countries, governments began to impose user fees for education and health services. In Kenya, citizens were invited to partner with the government in education through the construction of schools, first called Harambee schools and later Complementary schools.[7] In this partnership, communities would build schools and school facilities, and the government would supply teachers for the schools.[8] In this same period, there was an increased growth of urban informal settlements caused by massive rural–urban migration, which led to exponential growth of low-income and poor populations in urban areas.[9] These unplanned settlements occupied fallow government land and consequently had no supporting infrastructure or amenities, such as schools.[10]

The convergence of these two factors – the absence of government-led provision of education and the growth of urban informal settlements – resulted in a lacuna in the provision of basic education for the poor. Increasingly, various non-state providers came forward to offer education services. In the urban informal settlements, where some of the poorest populations dwell, these were mostly NGOs, faith- and community-based organisations and self-help groups. Other schools were started by private individuals, whether as a community endeavour or through entrepreneurial initiative. Many of these schools were unregistered while others were registered under various heterogeneous legal frameworks, such as through the State Law Office and the

6   Anne Nduta Gichuri, *The structural adjustment program and education reform in Kenya*, Minneapolis: University of Minnesota, 2006. Ministry of Education, Science and Technology, Kenya, Registration guidelines for Alternative Provision of Basic Education and Training (APBET), Nairobi, 2015. William C. Smith and Tony Baker, *From free to fee: Are for-profit, fee-charging private schools the solution for the world's poor?*, 2017, www.results.org/uploads/files/From_Free_to_Fee.pdf.
7   Ministry of Education, Science and Technology, Registration guidelines for APBET.
8   Gichuri, *The structural adjustment program*.
9   Benta A. Abuya, Kassahun Admassu, Moses Ngware, Elijah O. Onsomu and Moses Oketch, 'Free primary education and implementation in Kenya: the role of primary teachers in addressing the policy gap', *SAGE Open*, 2015.
10   Gichuri, *The structural adjustment program*. Moses Ngware, Benta A. Abuya, Kassahun Admassur, Maurice Mutisya, Peter Musyoka and Moses Oketch, *Quality and access to education in urban informal settlements in Kenya*, Nairobi: African Population and Health Research Center, 2013, http://aphrc.org/wp-content/uploads/2013/11/ERP-III-Report.pdf. Asayo Ohba, 'Do low-cost private school leavers in the informal settlement have a good chance of admission to a government secondary school? A study from Kibera in Kenya', *Compare: A Journal of Comparative and International Education*, 43 (2013): 763–82.

Department of Social Services, but not with the Ministry of Education. This means that these schools went unnoticed and unrecognised in government education circles for decades such that, first, their existence and data were not captured and, second, they could not be properly regulated by the Ministry of Education.[11] It was not until 2009 that the ministry established frameworks for registration and regulation of these types of schools.[12]

These schools, which mostly offer early childhood and primary-level education, have grown as multiple challenges have plagued the public provision of basic education. This growth was hastened by the implementation of the Free Primary Education policy in 2003 by the National Rainbow Coalition (NARC) government.[13] While encouraged by the global Education for All agenda, the quality of learning suffered as the influx of children into public primary schools was not met by the requisite government response.[14] These cumulative systemic challenges have manifested in poor learning outcomes in public primary schools. The Uwezo reports observe that 'there is still no significant improvement in learning outcomes: only 3 out of 10 children in Class 3 can do Class 2 work. On average, 1 out of 10 children in Kenyan primary schools are completing Class 8 without having acquired the basic competencies expected of a child completing Class 2'.[15] This situation, coupled with chronic teacher absenteeism,[16] has bolstered the narrative that public primary schools do not work and, accordingly, that there should be a space for private providers to

[11] Ministry of Education, Science and Technology, Registration guidelines for APBET.

[12] Nairobi City County, *Taskforce on the improvement of performance of public primary schools and transition rate from primary to secondary education in the Nairobi City County*, 2014, http://dialogues.sidint.net/downloads/MatungaTaskforceNairobiEducationReport2014.pdf.

[13] Ministry of Education, *A policy framework for education: Aligning education and training to the Constitution of Kenya (2010) and Kenya Vision 2030 and beyond*, 2012, www.tvetauthority.go.ke/downloads/Acts&Regulations/SESSIONAL_PAPER_%20No%2014%202012.pdf

[14] Daniel N. Sifuna, 'The challenge of increasing access and improving quality: an analysis of universal primary education interventions in Kenya and Tanzania since the 1970s', *International Review of Education*, 536 (2007).

[15] Uwezo, *Are our children learning? Uwezo Kenya 6th learning assessment report*, 2016, www.twaweza.org/uploads/files/UwezoKenya2015ALAReport-FINAL-EN-web.pdf.

[16] Tessa Bold, Mwangi Kimenyi, Germano Mwabu and Justin Sandefur, *The high return to low-cost private schooling in a developing country*, Africa Growth Initiative Working Papers, No. 5, 2013, www.cgdev.org/files/1425807%7B_%7Dfile%7B_%7DSandefur%7B_%7Det%7B_%7Dal%7B_%7DHigh%7B_%7Dreturn%7B_%7DFINAL.pdf.

offer equal or better quality learning, especially for poor people unable to access the luxury of higher end private schools for themselves. This position grounds and seemingly gives legitimacy to the private sector's mandate to advance the commercialisation of education. Low-fee private schools position themselves as meeting the growing demand for education that the government has been unable to supply.

For-profit low-fee private schools target the poor by introducing relatively low user fees. The fees are generally charged termly, but parents tend to default in payment and, although their children are not excluded from school for non-payment of fees,[17] most of the schools expect full payment before the end of the school term.[18] For-profit low-fee private schools often employ untrained and unqualified teachers and have poor-quality facilities.[19] However, the illusion of accountability to parents, which is premised on the argument that parents understand the nuances of school choice and know how to critically evaluate and select schools that offer the best quality, tends to ensure better teacher attendance as they fear losing their jobs.[20] Many low-fee private schools lack security of land tenure and have no legally enforceable rental contract, aggravated by cash-flow challenges experienced as a result of the financial constraints on parents unable to pay the fees.[21] Despite the 2009 policy by the Ministry of Education, many of these schools continue to be unregistered[22] and exist outside of the national

[17] Pauline Rose and Modupe Adelabu, 'Private sector contributions to education for all in Nigeria', in Prachi Srivastava and Geoffrey Walford (eds), *Private schooling in less economically developed countries: Asian and African perspectives*, Oxford: Symposium Books, 2007, pp 67–87.

[18] Joanna Härmä and Folasade Adefisayo, 'Scaling up: the challenges facing low-fee private schools in the slums of Lagos, Nigeria', in Prachi Srivastava (ed.), *Low-fee private schooling: Aggravating equity or mitigating disadvantage*, Oxford: Symposium Books, 2013.

[19] Stephen P. Heyneman and Jonathan M.B. Stern, 'Low cost private schools for the poor: what public policy is appropriate?', *International Journal of Educational Development*, 35 (2014): 3–15.

[20] Joanna Härmä, 'Access or quality? Why do families living in slums choose low-cost private schools in Lagos, Nigeria?', *Oxford Review of Education*, 39 (2013): 548–66.

[21] James Tooley, Pauline Dixon and Olanrewaju Olaniyan, 'Private and public schooling in low-income areas of Lagos state, Nigeria: a census and comparative survey', *International Journal of Educational Research*, 43 (2005), 125–46.

[22] Laura Day Ashley, Claire Mcloughlin, Monazza Aslam, Jakob Engel, Joseph Wales, Shenila Rawal and others, *The role and impact of private schools in developing countries: Education rigorous literature review*, London: DFID (Department for International Development), 2014, http://r4d.dfid.gov.uk/.

education regulatory frameworks. They can do this with impunity as the government lacks capacity to enforce the regulations.[23]

Based on this burgeoning growth, low-fee private school chains entered the education market in some African countries to take advantage of the opportunities presented by the shortcomings in public education systems. They operate under the same regulatory framework as the smaller low-fee private schools and there is a similar concern about a lack of accountability for the performance of low-fee private school chains. In contrast to small low-fee private schools, however, the chains are very well resourced and organised, and function according to a business model aimed at making a profit through economies of scale. For them, the challenges in the education system offer a lucrative business opportunity while also fulfilling a social need. The strength of low-fee private school chains lies in standardising a model of education and proliferating quickly, and, in this sense, the educational and regulatory concerns about them may differ. Due to their founding objectives and scale of operations, they are on a different level to the smaller low-fee private schools. Despite these distinct concerns, they have found a market and are meeting a need for learners, with one chain in Kenya reporting that they have opened at least 400 schools since 2009 and 520 schools globally.[24]

Meanwhile, the debate about whether low-fee private schools and chains are successful in offering better access to quality education than public schools rages on. The rigorous review of low-fee private schools commissioned by the United Kingdom's Department for International Development (DFID)[25] makes the case that there are several variables to consider in making such a judgment, but in sum, they may not be delivering better quality education. The review points to evidence that low-fee private schools are facing considerable challenges: weak accountability to parents, uncertainty about the sustainability of their model as it is questionable whether poor families can continue to pay for education, and limited geographical reach as they tend to serve the urban poor at the expense of rural poor, who are the most socioeconomically marginalised in the education system. In this regard, a study by Harma[26] points out that the further one is from an urban

[23] Day Ashley et al, *The role and impact of private schools in developing countries*. Heyneman and Stern, 'Low cost private schools for the poor …'.

[24] Bridge International Academies website, www.bridgeinternationalacademies.com.

[25] Day Ashley et al, *The role and impact of private schools in developing countries*.

[26] Joanna Härmä, 'School choice in rural Nigeria? The limits of low-fee private schooling in Kwara state', *Comparative Education*, 52 (2016): 246–66.

centre, the less likely it is there will be a low-fee private school. The DFID review also casts doubt on whether low-fee private schools are equally accessible to boys and girls and, perhaps most troubling, it further finds that low-fee private schools are in fact more expensive than state schools. All of these problems are compounded by ineffective state regulation. There have been criticisms of the DFID rigorous review, focusing on its methodology which impacts its findings, from Tooley and Longfield.[27]

There is also significant difficulty in determining the number of APBET schools in Kenya because, as mentioned before, many are still unregistered and those that are registered are still spread around the jurisdiction of various state agencies rather than under the oversight of the Ministry of Education. In determining the proliferation of APBET schools, studies have relied on the number of students or parents who self-report as attending or paying for APBET schools.[28] One such study in Kenya indicates that overall, 53% of the children were enrolled in government schools. In Nairobi, Mombasa and Eldoret slums, however, about 58% of the children attended non-government schools as reflected in Figure 1.

[27] J. Tooley and D. Longfield *The Role and Impact of Private Schools in Developing Countries: A response to the DFID-commissioned Rigorous Review*, London, 2015. Pearson. Retrieved from http://eprint.ncl.ac.uk/file_store/production/208667/ DEA1EDE1-4499-49D6-A971-C0128AB3F19C.pdf

[28] Ngware et al, Quality and access to education in urban informal settlements in Kenya. Moses Oketch, Maurice Mutisya, Moses Ngware and Alex C. Ezeh, 'Why are there proportionately more poor pupils enrolled in non-state schools in urban Kenya in spite of FPE policy?', *International Journal of Education Development*, 30 (2010): 23–32.

Figure 1: Distribution of schools in urban slums in Kenya

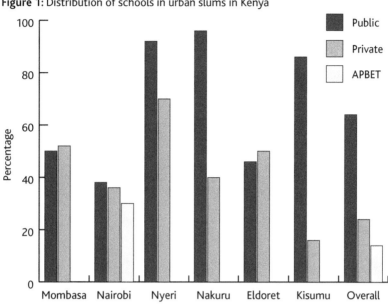

Source: Data from M. Ngware, B. A. Abuya, K. Admassu, M. Mutisya, P. Musyoka and M. Oketch (2013)
Quality and access to education in urban informal settlements in Kenya, Nairobi: African Population and
Health Research Center, 2013, http://aphrc.org/wp-content/uploads/2013/11/ERP-III-Report.pdf

The study argues that these varying patterns of attendance reflect
the differing perceptions of the quality of public schools, such that
public schools are the yardstick for gauging success rather than the
pariah they are made out to be by champions of the marketisation of
education.[29] The study also suggests that a shortage of public schools in
densely populated informal urban settlements has led to more children
attending APBET schools.

Nairobi City County convened a taskforce in 2014 to carry out
an evaluation of the schools in the county. It found that it had 1,724
APBET schools, with 498,734 learners, 16,516 teaching staff and
4,448 support staff. Additionally, in a census done between November
2013 and January 2014, 300 APBET schools had registered 8,820
candidates for the primary school national examinations, known as the
Kenya Certificate of Primary Education (KCPE) and had 592 schools

---

[29] Ngware et al, *Quality and access to education in urban informal settlements in Kenya*.
James Tooley, *The beautiful tree: A personal journey into how the world's poorest people
are educating themselves*, Washington, DC: Cato Institute, 2009, http://solo.bodleian.
ox.ac.uk/OXVU1:oxfaleph020424818.

registered as KCPE examination centres.[30] The estimated figures and the data from the studies mentioned above suggest there has been a progressive growth in the numbers of non-state schools.

Regulation of low-fee private schools in Kenya

The rigorous review commissioned by DFID points to the need for a greater understanding of the influence of the 'political and market conditions within which education providers operate, and the effects of the relationship between the public and private sectors'.[31] This section explores this question from both a global and national perspective to reflect on and traverse the regulatory issues that arise.

The global outlook

International and regional instruments have long been established to govern the right to education. These include Article 26 of the Universal Declaration of Human Rights (UDHR), Article 13 of the United Nations International Covenant on Economic, Social and Cultural Rights (ICESCR) and Article 11 of the African Charter on the Rights and Welfare of the Child, among others.[32] The United Nations Committee on Economic, Social and Cultural Rights (CESCR), in its General Comment No. 13, has developed standards to be met by state parties to the ICESCR in the provision of the right to education. These essential standards relate to the availability, accessibility, acceptability and adaptability of education.

Global efforts to realise the right to education have been bolstered by the 1990 Education for All initiative. This is a global initiative welcoming the commitments made by the international community premised on a rights-based approach to education. This collective commitment to achieving education for 'every citizen in every society'

---

[30] Nairobi City County, *Taskforce on the improvement of performance of public primary schools.*

[31] Day Ashley et al, *The role and impact of private schools in developing countries.*

[32] These include: the UNESCO Convention against Discrimination in Education (1960), the International Covenant on the Elimination of All Forms of Racial Discrimination (1965), the Convention on the Elimination of All Forms of Discrimination against Women (1979), the African Charter on Human and People's Rights (1987), the Convention on the Rights of the Child (1989), the International Convention on the Protection of the Rights of All Migrant Workers and Members of Their Families (1990), the Convention on the Rights of Persons with Disabilities (2006).

was reinforced at the World Forum on Education in Dakar in 2000.[33] Through the Millennium Development Goals and now the Sustainable Development Goals, states are working to achieve inclusive and quality learning for all (Goal 4).

These legal and political promises come with financial implications for developing countries. In the Kenyan context, the state would not be able to achieve these goals without donor support. The global agenda has shifted during this time according to the geopolitical considerations at play and the varied interests of different countries giving aid to Kenya.[34] These shifts have had varied consequences for Kenya. The aid journey began with the implementation of the Marshall Plan in the 1960s, through to the post-independence giving of aid for ideological advantage in the battle between the capitalist West and socialist counterparts. It further developed in the structural adjustment programmes in the 1980s imposed by the World Bank and IMF due to rising corruption, and then aid was used to push for democracy and better governance in the 1990s.[35] The Accra Plan of 2005 and the Paris Declaration of 2015 brought a new approach to aid and development in education, laying out three principles for investment and engagement with recipient countries: harmonisation, alignment and managing for results.[36]

The implications of the aid agenda and the power dynamic it represents are pertinent. The exercise of this power in relation to regulation is central to the growth of low-fee private schools. This is particularly clear where aid agencies give financing to low-fee private schools, as they could exercise their influence to shape regulation in order to promote donor agencies' national interests and agendas.[37] An apt example is a chain in Kenya which is funded by various European government aid agencies, as well as famous entrepreneurs, which

---

[33] UNESCO, *World Education Forum, Dakar, Senegal, 26–28 April 2000: Final Report; 2000*, Paris: UNESCO, 2000, http://unesdoc.unesco.org/images/0012/001211/121117e.pdf.

[34] Mario Novelli, 'The new geopolitics of educational aid: from cold wars to holy wars?', *International Journal of Educational Development*, 30 (2010): 453–9.

[35] Christopher Colclough and Andrew Webb, 'A triumph of hope over reason? Aid accords and education policy in Kenya', *Comparative Education*, 48 (2012): 263–80.

[36] Christopher Colclough, Kenneth King and Simon McGrath, 'The new politics of aid to education', *International Journal of Educational Development*, 30 (2010): 451–2. Liesbet Steer and Cecilie Wathne, 'Donor financing of basic education: opportunities and constraints', *International Journal of Educational Development*, 30 (2010): 472–80.

[37] Novelli, 'The new geopolitics of educational aid'. Colclough et al, 'The new politics of aid to education'.

gives the chain legitimacy and which is used to create regulations that favour the chain rather than the learner. There are multiple and at times competing interests in the regulatory discourse and this influences everything from the conceptualisation of the regulations to their implementation. Indeed, he who pays the piper calls the tune, but when the piper becomes a juke box, the competing interests pose challenges for the regulator.

National regulatory framework for APBET schools

Low-fee private schools and chains view regulation as overly cumbersome, unnecessarily restrictive and exploited by enforcers as an opportunity to collect bribes.[38] Where adherence to state regulation is weak, corruption has the chance to thrive. Heyneman and Stern[39] say that 'The key question is how to effectively regulate without placing counter-productive constraints on flexibility and creativity, the essential elements in the non-state school sector.' Smuts' chapter in this collection offers a best practice model that shows some promise of this in South Africa. The structure around regulating APBET schools revolves around incorporation of the schools, registration with the appropriate education agencies, licensing by county government authorities and taxation. The 2015 APBET guidelines,[40] which are based on the APBET Policy 2009, are the principal legal instruments used to govern APBET schools, and were the first attempt to recognise low-fee private schools, synthesise the issues that arise in their regulation and also identify the areas in which certain tensions may develop. Three pertinent areas for regulation emerge from the guidelines and their comparison with the provisions of the Basic Education Act, 2013 and the Basic Education Regulations, 2015; these are teacher qualifications, registration of APBET schools and the curriculum offered in these schools.

The registration of schools is a big challenge for the Ministry of Education because some schools are registered as NGOs, charities or even orphanages, under different legal frameworks, making it difficult to apply the education regulations to them in a uniform manner. The consolidation of registration requirement in the 2015 guidelines was necessary so that all those schools not registered would thereafter have

---

[38] Heyneman and Stern, 'Low cost private schools for the poor'.
[39] Heyneman and Stern, 'Low cost private schools for the poor'.
[40] Ministry of Education, Science and Technology, Registration guidelines for APBET.

an opportunity to be registered under the guidelines promulgated by the Ministry of Education.

Furthermore, a major barrier to registration stems from the land requirements in the regulations. No school can be registered if it lacks an identifiable location. Many of the APBET schools are squatters on government land and so do not have a lease for the land or a title to the property. They are unable to meet the requirement and remain unregistered. Those that are not squatters might still not have lease agreements as they often informally rent spaces from churches and other organisations to use during the week. The requirement for title and leases incurs an expense that may be beyond the financial capacity of these schools. Therefore, there are powerful incentives for them to avoid registration.

Obtaining registration for APBET schools is also not straightforward. The promulgation of the APBET Registration Guidelines, 2015, immediately deregistered all APBET schools, leading to the landmark case, *Republic v The County Education Board & another Ex-parte Bridge International Academies Ltd, Judicial Review No. 3 of 2016*.[41] In this case, the County Education Board of Busia County in Western Kenya closed 50 schools based on the stipulation for automatic deregistration and re-registration under the 2015 guidelines. These schools were operated by Bridge International Academies, a major chain of low-fee private schools that emerged in Kenya in 2009 and has spread across country. The County Education Board in Busia County wrote to Bridge International Academies requiring them to close all the schools that had not been re-registered. The government had given the schools two years to re-register, even though they should have been immediately shut down for failing to comply with the 2015 guidelines. Bridge International Academies appealed to the court to keep their schools open. The court decided against Bridge International Academies (except in respect of two schools that were in the process of re-registration). The court affirmed the role of the County Education Board to enforce the guidelines. This demonstrates adherence to a strict enforcement approach by the courts. The court was also sensitive to the right to education of the learners when crafting a remedy. It ordered that the closure of the unregistered Bridge International Academies schools happens at the end of the school term and that students in those schools be reassigned to new schools by the government.

---

[41] [2017] eKLR.

The guidelines also set uniform standards for APBET schools.[42] First, they attempt to standardise and improve school infrastructure and the curriculum. The challenge here is that there is a special curriculum to be implemented for APBET schools. Notwithstanding this, most APBET schools deliver the standard curriculum and not the specific APBET curriculum. This reflects their market-oriented approach to education in responding to parents' desire for their children to pass examinations under the regular national system. There is also little pressure on these schools to comply with the curriculum standards specifically set for them.

The Basic Education Regulations, 2015 address teacher training. Regulation 49 provides that all persons deployed to teach in basic education schools of learning and training shall be required to have undertaken a training programme approved or recognised by the Cabinet Secretary and to be registered with the Teachers Service Commission. This stands in stark contrast with the provisions of the 2015 APBET guidelines, which only require that 30% of teachers in APBET schools be trained and qualified, with the remaining 70% to be progressively trained and eventually registered.

Discussion on the regulation of APBET schools

Ideological approach and negotiated boundaries

Two ideologies, and therefore also two corresponding regulatory approaches, predominate in the discourse on managing APBET schools. The first is a neoliberal ideology that manifests as support for increased privatisation. The privatisation, commercialisation or marketisation of education aims to introduce market models into the education system and is fits into the theoretical framework of economic neoliberalism.[43] Rather than undertaking a positive obligation to fund and provide education, the state assumes the role of 'coordinator of coordination', in line with managerialism, such that it does not have a role in the actual delivery of learning but rather only in the management of those who deliver learning.[44] This leads to a multiplication of centres of power and decision making, giving rise to constant negotiation and

[42]   Ministry of Education, Science and Technology, Registration guidelines for APBET.
[43]   Maia Chankseliani, 'Are we using Friedman's roadmap? A comparative analysis of stimuli of private school enrolments in post-Soviet countries', *International Journal of Educational Development*, 38 (2014): 13–21.
[44]   Balarin, 'The changing governance of education'.

renegotiation of policy, law and standards to accommodate different ideologies and approaches.

The education challenges in Kenya can be framed as a supply and demand issue in which the privatisation of education targets the urban poor where there is limited access to public education. The poor cannot turn to public schools because they are few, poorly resourced and suffer teacher absenteeism.[45] In a desire to obtain a quality education for their children they turn to the private sector where they are compelled to pay for services that are similar to or worse than public services in the hope that they will eke value out of the low-fee private schools and chains. As already noted, it is important to acknowledge that the rise of privatisation has links to foreign aid and business interests.[46]

A human rights-based approach to education, on the other hand, is anchored in the centrality of the state's accountability for the delivery of education. Unlike market approaches, which place emphasis on profits and meeting market demands, a human rights-based approach requires that every person is equally able to access quality education. Rights-holders can assert a breach of their rights and hold the duty bearer accountable. A human rights-based approach throws into sharp relief the challenges that the government faces regarding the lack of resources, personnel, technical capacity and universal political capital across regulatory bodies mandated with the management of education to achieve these standards.

Accordingly, the differing ideological inclinations of various stakeholders towards APBET schools go to the root of their legitimacy and their role in education. The government believes that APBET schools are a temporary alternative which does not deserve long-term investment, whereas the private sector believes that they should be allowed to do as they wish because they are serving the poor. This poses a challenge for regulation and policy making, because stakeholders come to the table with very different approaches to the same issues, leading to tensions and conflicts.[47] As such, the rise of APBET schools requires a unique response that both supports them and keeps them in check.[48] This nuanced position is captured by the concept of 'negotiated boundaries'.

---

[45] Bold et al, *The high return to low-cost private schooling in a developing country*.

[46] Novelli, 'The new geopolitics of educational aid'.

[47] Daniel Fiorino, 'Regulatory negotiation as a form of public participation', in Ortwin Renn, Thomas Webler and Peter Wiedemann (eds) *Fairness and competence in citizen participation*, Dordrecht: Kluwer, 1995, pp 223–7.

[48] Robert L. Sachs, 'An alternative to the traditional rulemaking process: a case study of negotiation in the development of regulations', *Villanova Law Review*, 29 (1983).

The idea behind negotiated boundaries is that where the human rights-based and neoliberal approaches to education encounter each other, a conflict ensues which must be mediated through various processes to the benefit of the learner. This occurs where expectations flowing from the right to education clash with limitations in the implementation of education and the advancement of private sector efforts to participate in an education 'market', leading to a negotiation. In this scenario, regulation, as a process, aims to facilitate positive outcomes for all parties to the benefit of children in schools.

This rationale of compromise, which underpins the concept of negotiated boundaries, manifests in how the APBET Registration Guidelines, 2015, deviate from the provisions of the Basic Education Act, 2013 and the Basic Education Regulations, 2015. The structure and approach of the APBET Registration Guidelines, 2015, demonstrates that a compromise is at play in delivering education to the poor, perhaps best exemplified in the provisions on teacher training. It has also manifested in the circumvention of regulations in ways that have sometimes led to corruption.[49]

With the risks associated with these compromises in mind, how should regulation respond to the concept of negotiated boundaries? First, the concept of negotiated boundaries underscores the importance of developing a realistic regulatory approach which takes account of the limitations of all stakeholders,[50] given their competing interests, incentives and obligations: the government's duty to provide and regulate education, the rights of children to enjoy access to quality education, and the non-state actor's agenda in supporting education through either for-profit or non-profit means.[51]

Second, the concept of negotiated boundaries draws our attention to the varying ideologies and cultures relevant to the regulation of education provision.[52] This invites debate about political and philosophical considerations as well as an awareness of any cultural dynamics that might affect decision making and regulation. This must be taken into consideration in relation to both the regulator and the regulated, as well as any other stakeholders involved.

[49] Heyneman and Stern, 'Low cost private schools for the poor'.

[50] Barry M. Mitnick, 'Regulation and the theory of agency', *Review of Policy Research*, 1 (1982): 442–53.

[51] Philip J. Harter, 'Assessing the assessors: the actual performance of negotiated rulemaking', *New York University Environmental Law Review*, 2000: 32–59.

[52] Daniel J. Fiorino, 'Regulatory negotiation as a policy process', *Public Administration Review*, 48 (1988): 764–72.

In sum, the concept of negotiated boundaries highlights the importance of regulatory discourse that recognises the legal and power structures and sub-structures at play in the provision of education. It requires a regulatory system where competing interests, incentives and obligations are clarified, where all stakeholders are consulted, and where outcomes are consolidated in a plan that must be implemented.[53]

Silence, inclusion, voice and agency

A major challenge in addressing the proliferation of APBET schools is the fact that, from the 1980s, the government had neither a policy nor guidelines for them, which allowed their proliferation to go unchecked until 2009. Furthermore, there are no official data records for APBET schools, with the upshot that deliberations about them are based on estimates rather than accurate figures, which only compounds the lack of regulation. Patent negligence by the government has allowed these schools to thrive unchecked. Although this has created opportunities for prosperity for private actors with entrepreneurial initiative, it has also meant that those private actors who are not providing quality education are not monitored and held accountable – not even those who may be involved in illegal activity are rooted out. This has left children of the urban poor – the ultimate recipients of this education – vulnerable to abuse of various kinds. The introduction of various levels of regulation, from incorporation to registration and licensing, are intended to ensure that all APBET schools are monitored. Yet as they stand, the regulations are not positioned to make much of a difference in light of the shortcomings identified earlier. Moreover, Mcloughlin[54] points out that the enforcement of regulations remains a challenge because of the government's lack of capacity (in terms of both financial and social capital) and the absence of strong incentives to enforce them.

Inequality and inequity also play a significant role in the regulation of APBET schools in relation to the education of the poor. As equality in education is a central part of the aspirations of human rights-based approaches to education and the Sustainable Development Goals, it should be a key focus of regulation to ensure that all learners are

---

[53] Harter, 'Assessing the assessors'.

[54] Claire Mcloughlin, 'Low-cost private schools: evidence, approaches and emerging issues', London: Overseas Development Institute, 2013, www.enterprise-development.org/wp-content/uploads/Low-cost_private_schools.pdf.

allowed equal opportunities for access to quality learning.[55] In spite of this mandate, however, there is silence around issues relating to gender, special needs learners and out-of-school learners. The APBET Registration Guidelines, 2015, as they stand, do not offer a solution for the inclusion of these learners, nor do they ensure that these learners enjoy quality learning.[56] Accordingly, the silence on these issues amounts to consent to their neglect. Furthermore, the APBET Registration Guidelines, 2015, set lower or different standards for curriculum, teacher training and infrastructure, in contrast to the Basic Education Act, 2013 and Basic Education Regulations, 2015. They effectively become discriminatory towards the poor who are the main target for these schools. This perpetuates socioeconomic discrimination as it results in learners from poor families and poor learners receiving a lower or different quality of education from those who attend public schools. The regulation of private education providers must be pro-poor and inclusive of different identity groups, for example, girls. Research shows that household wealth determines access to quality education[57] and that female children face greater barriers to accessing education than their male counterparts.[58]

The development of regulations requires an inclusive and representative process if the regulations themselves are to present a useful solution for all stakeholders. The fact that the government does not have any comprehensive or accurate data on APBET schools means the direct participation of these providers is key to avoiding a scenario in which a set of guidelines is issued while providers continue to avoid, ignore or be ignorant of them.

---

[55] Pauline Rose, 'Equity in education post-2015: how do we get there?', World Education Blog, 20 February 2013, https://gemreportunesco.wordpress.com/2013/02/20/equity-in-education-post-2015-how-do-we-get-there/.

[56] Joanna Härmä, 'Low cost private schooling in India: is it pro poor and equitable?', *International Journal of Educational Development*, 31 (2011), 350–6. Keith M. Lewin, *Educational access, equity, and development: Planning to make right realities*, Paris: UNESCO, 2015.

[57] Keith M. Lewin, *The limits to growth of non-government private schooling in sub Saharan Africa*, Research Monograph No. 5, Brighton: University of Sussex, 2007, http://www.create-rpc.org/pdf_documents/PTA5.pdf.

[58] Joanna Härmä, 'Is low-fee private primary schooling affordable for the poor? Evidence from rural India', in Susan Robertson, Karen Mundy, and Antoni Verger (eds), *Public–private partnerships in education*, Cheltenham: Edward Elgar, 2012, pp 243–57. Elaine Unterhalter, 'Poverty, education, gender and the Millennium Development Goals: reflections on boundaries and intersectionality', *Theory and Research in Education*, 10 (2012).

Regulation not only clarifies the issues at hand but also offers a voice to the various stakeholders. The process of regulation crystallises the competing ideologies, agendas and interests of the people around the table, and ensures they are all given due consideration. Without agency, however, a balanced agenda cannot be set, as those without the requisite clout – either through direct or representative participation – will not have a voice to address their concerns, with the result that the regulations may be developed to their detriment.[59] The corollary of this is that those who are present during the development of regulations exercise considerable influence over what makes it into the regulations. If these powerful voices are not representative of those affected by the regulations, then the regulations themselves would not meet their goal of determining negotiated boundaries. Additionally, foreign aid agencies and investors in education have the obligation to participate in ensuring that equity and social justice are prioritised and secured through the regulatory process. Given that many APBET schools and chains are supported through finances from these agencies and investors, they have to bear some of the responsibility of making sure that these schools adhere to human rights standards to the greatest extent possible.

Bearing this in mind, a key question is how decisions on the education of the poor are made. Do they have agency to decide how they are educated, if others determine the kind and quality of learning they get? The argument has been made that low-fee private schools give the poor choice,[60] but the genuineness of this choice is questionable. Where organisations offer inferior-quality education while the government lacks the capacity to offer anything better in the public school system, the right to education fails to serve as a multiplier right that empowers the poor. Instead, their fate is to be locked into a cycle of poverty as they are forced to take what is offered instead of being allowed to expect better.

Conclusion

This chapter offers an insight into the social and economic context in which low-fee private schools operate in Kenya. It raises various concerns about low-fee private schools that are relevant to many countries, while specifically revealing how the Kenyan government has

---

[59] Fiorino, 'Regulatory negotiation as a form of public participation'.
[60] Harold Alderman, Peter F. Orazem and Elizabeth M. Paterno, 'School quality, school cost, and the public/private school choices of low-income households in Pakistan', *Journal of Human Resources*, 36 (2001).

approached them. It demonstrates that these schools have proliferated as a result of various global and domestic socio-legal and economic policies. This has led to the unintended consequence of legitimising a market for the provision of private education to the poor. As such, regulation is applied as a corrective rather than a pre-emptive measure, leading to reactive laws and policies rather than proactive ones. It also demonstrates the urgent need for the government not only to improve the regulatory process for APBET schools, but also to push forward its efforts to improve the quality of public education through increased investments in infrastructure, better equipment, and employing more teachers with better benefits.

The chapter argues that, in spite of the APBET guidelines promulgated in 2015, there remain challenges in ensuring accountability, equality before the law and the participation of all stakeholders in the regulation of low-fee private schools. The Kenyan government still does not know exactly how many APBET schools operate in the country and therefore cannot adequately regulate them. As demonstrated by the fragmentation in the regulation of these schools, it reveals that there is a need to consolidate the incorporation, registration, licensing and taxation regimes to ensure a uniform approach to law and policy on low-fee private schools. As such, a comprehensive overhaul of the regulation of APBET schools is required. This is certainly a future area for research in the regulation of privatisation of basic education, with the aim of proposing a framework for regulation. Sufficient data must be collected about these schools and appropriate and uniform strategies must be employed by the various government agencies and county governments to regulate them. If this is not achieved, the state risks failing to protect rights-holders from inequality in access to quality education, leaving the poor without any recourse against the APBET school owners. In pointing to some of the current loopholes in the regulation of low-fee private schools in Kenya, this study offers valuable insights for policy makers concerned with ensuring that the regulation of private education providers advances the right to education.

THREE

Education at the margins: the potential benefits of private educational initiatives for disadvantaged groups

Melanie Smuts

Introduction

Early morning in a messy, industrial zone of Johannesburg, children cross a disused park in yellow, green and grey t-shirts towards a big building that still looks like an old factory on their way to a colourful school sign that reads Jeppe Park Primary.[1] The area is known as Jeppestown – one of the oldest neighbourhoods in the city. It suffers from high rates of crime and a lack of investment in infrastructure. The streets are full of litter. The buildings mostly house car-parts dealers. Fires often break out in the trash-heaps in the park. It is not a friendly place for children.

Like so many sites of rapid urbanisation in Africa, this is exactly where families typically live as parents from rural areas move to cities in search of jobs.[2] Children here stay in abandoned warehouse spaces – where big floor sections are divided off from other families by scraps of fabric to create informal sleeping areas. Sometimes children will live in overcrowded apartments with sub-tenants crowding into the communal areas. Finding schools for children in areas such as Jeppestown is extremely difficult. Gauteng, the province in which Johannesburg is located, suffered a school shortage that resulted in 58,000 learners without a school to attend at the beginning of the

---

[1] See: www.streetlightschools.org/streetlightjeppestown.
[2] Urban populations across Africa are projected to grow by 473% in the period 1995 to 2025, http://web.mit.edu/urbanupgrading/upgrading/case-examples/overview-africa/regional-overview.html.

school year in 2017.[3] At the closest local public school in Jeppestown, the waiting list in Grade 1 runs to over 222 pupils. They had to be turned away at the beginning of the school year in 2016. The public system is simply not able to meet the needs of learners and ensure access to school for all.

The children in the colourful t-shirts crossing the park are an exception to these statistics. They enter the glass doors of the factory building and enter into a beautiful educational facility. Two years before, the school was a disused industrial space – blacked out and broken windows, cold concrete floors and broken lights. Now, it is a school that contains indoor slides, play-walls, purpose-built classrooms, fantasy corners, a dining hall, an auditorium and a playground.[4] It is a school run by a Streetlight Schools, a non-profit organisation aiming to address the lack of access to quality education for learners in South Africa. After six months, learners in this school academically outperform the average South African pupil by several months compared to the standard set by the state curriculum.[5] At Jeppe Park Primary, children who are being failed by the state system receive – for a cost equivalent to the provincial per pupil spending average – educational outcomes that are normally reserved for the very rich. Parents pay R495 (approximately 30GBP) a month in school fees, heavily subsidised through rental cuts by the building owner, donations from local businesses and grants by foundations.

This intervention is successful for a number of reasons: it is responsive to the context of the particular community, it is cost-effective, it is adaptable (the school timetable has changed over 45 times over the past year to adjust to the needs of learners and parents), and it is run by a combination of talented local educators and experienced experts who constantly receive professional development and feedback on their work.

The founding of the first Streetlight School in Jeppestown is a positive measure to address a complex problem that manifests in different ways around the world, but at its root is a state system that has not met the educational needs and demands of a rapidly changing society. This, in

---

[3] See 'Gauteng's education department breaks promise to Constitutional Court', www.businesslive.co.za/bd/national/education/2017-01-10-gautengs-education-department-breaks-promise-to-constitutional-court/.

[4] See 'Jeppe Park Primary becomes living laboratory', http://alive2green.com/jeppe-park-primary-becomes-living-laboratory-green-schools/.

[5] See: www.streetlightschools.org/blog/2016/8/16/6-months-of-student-progress-a-review

turn, leads to private innovations from the ground up that often help achieve the advancement of access to quality education for all.

This challenges the dominant narrative in human rights-based practice and research that private providers undermine the right to education. There are cogent and compelling reasons to critique the advent of private operators in education, but there is no room to adequately address that debate here. This chapter merely outlines how it is not a simple or binary question that 'private is better than public', but rather illuminates the factors that have led to private actors getting involved, and outlines where they have had success: through breaking ground for marginalised learners to be educated, by being the sites of invention of innovative pedagogies and, in more recent times, finding ways to make education more cost-effective. This could be a blueprint for solving the systemic problems in the public system. At the same time, the emergence of private school operators is not a passing trend, and we need to explore what best practices can be developed to ensure this emerging sector upholds the right to education so learners can meaningfully access educational opportunities.

The benefit of educational approaches and schools that have operated outside the formal state system extends beyond the individual institutions themselves to the broader debate about how we conceptualise and enforce education as a right. Four critical ways in which private operators have positively influenced the public sector include:

- recognising the equality of individuals;
- undoing the legacies of racism, sexism and colonialism;
- developing pedagogical strategies;
- and, perhaps controversially, playing a collaborative role in creating more innovative ways of providing cost-effective education.

The common thread among these four aspects – across the world and specifically in South Africa – is that non-state operators often envisage an improved future state of education that can reinvigorate the public system with new ideas and in turn benefit education systems overall.

Before turning to examine the multiple ways in which the private sector can assist in realising a right to education, it is helpful to pause and consider the different character of various private actors. And though this article defends the role of private actors in education, it does not defend all forms of privatisation. A key distinction in this regard is between for-profit and not-for-profit private providers of education. Many others have written on the dangers of low-cost, for-profit education and this article will not attempt to add to that commentary. This may change in future, but from the examples we currently have, the more relevant distinction is arguably not state versus non-state but rather for-profit versus not-for-profit.[6]

It is by no means clear that for-profit education, and in particular for-profit education subsidised by states as well as corporate forms of low-cost for-profit models, have produced any positive results. Neither is it clear that the harm caused by extracting profit from education provision can be justified with reference to any countervailing benefits. There is little or no evidence that privatisation adds meaningfully to the education sector where it is driven by financial interests.[7] This is why a more nuanced understanding of the different forms of private education is valuable: to identify where private initiatives could benefit the system overall through improved outcomes, new tools for learning or more culturally sensitive forms of school management.

Education systems would suffer if inventions and interventions on the margins were not allowed to flourish. Overlooking the value of facilitating diverse approaches would leave education systems around the world far poorer, and would severely hamper our ability to imagine new and increasingly better forms of education provision. Below I consider how non-profit private providers can positively contribute to upholding the right to education by looking at: the equality of individuals; overcoming the legacies of racism, sexism and colonialism; pedagogical innovations; and collaborative and cost-effective investment in education.

The equality of individuals

There are very few examples where states were the first to give girls, black children, slaves, children of lower castes, children with disabilities, or refugee and migrant children access to education. Such initiatives were often first undertaken by Church institutions, community organisations, education pioneers and philanthropists. In South Africa, this tradition has been particularly important as the mission schools contributed valuably to the education of black learners who became

---

[6]   For a broader discussion on the issue of profit in education see Martha C. Nussbaum, *Not for profit: Why democracy needs the humanities*, Princeton: Princeton University Press, 2016.

[7]   The most controversial example is Bridge International Academies, which has created an outcry among international education experts and local governments alike. See: www.theguardian.com/global-development/2016/nov/04/judge-orders-closure-low-cost-bridge-international-academies-uganda.

the political class that led the liberation struggle. And, despite many of the problematic elements of mission schools, they were still the only places where black learners could receive an education. The founders, as well as all of the major leaders of the African National Congress – including John Dube, Albert Luthuli, Nelson Mandela, Walter Sisulu and Oliver Tambo – were educated at a small handful of mission schools. This demonstrates the positive political component that non-state education can potentially provide to marginalised and disadvantaged learners, as was the case in colonial and Apartheid South Africa where racism and inequality negatively affected the rights of certain groups to state education.

Overcoming the legacies of racism, sexism and colonialism

Sadly, the colonial and Apartheid legacies continue to haunt South Africa. There are many current examples of discrimination in the public education system that speak to the deep and entrenched nature of legacies of racism, sexism and colonialism that undermine the right to education. Recently, there were protests at a local public girls' school against the requirement in the school code of conduct that black girls chemically straighten their hair.[8] Black hair in its natural form was considered 'unkempt' and prohibited by the school rules. This was a perfect storm of race, gender and colonial attitudes, but these legacies are arguably more pervasive in countries that inherited their public education system from colonial powers or oppressive regimes, such as in South Africa and India. These lingering forms of discrimination find expression in a range of school practices, from uniforms to punishment mechanisms that do not reflect the humanist ambitions of a right to education in a pluralistic society.

School-specific interventions and innovations on how to build better structures for teaching and learning can play a vital role in forming locally relevant solutions to such challenges, which can then grow upwards and outwards. Fostering these forms of innovation and problem solving is vital for achieving the broader goal of a right to education, although with the caveat that this still requires the careful management of types of private actors who have a role in the delivery of education rather than simply backing a public school system wholesale.

---

[8] 'Pretoria Girls High School pupil: I was instructed to fix myself as if I was broken', http://mg.co.za/article/2016-08-29-pretoria-girls-high-school-pupil-i-was-instructed-to-fix-myself-as-if-i-was-broken.

Pedagogical innovations from the margins

Pedagogically, non-state education has also been a powerful driver for innovation and improvement in education that has often extended into public school systems decades later. Maria Montessori, perhaps the most famous education reformer of the modern era, developed her educational approach at her Casa dei Bambini, which was created for low-income families in San Lorenzo, on the outskirts of Rome.[9] More than a century later, her work remains some of the most widely respected thinking on early childhood development. John Dewey, America's most renowned education thinker and reformer, began his famous Laboratory School in Chicago to experiment with what a democratic school system would look like.[10] The Waldorf School –the world-recognised educational approach developed by philosopher Rudolph Steiner – is named 'Waldorf' because the first school of this type was founded for the children of employees of the Waldorf-Astoria cigarette factory in Stuttgart.[11] Many Waldorf schools are now publicly funded and the movement has had a major influence on European education. The Reggio Emilia approach, founded in the town of the same name in Italy after the Second World War, essentially began as a community peace-building project run by a local teacher, and has attracted immense international interest recently.[12] In modern times, peripheral new schools in the US have been doing experimental and highly valuable work on introducing technology, building critical thinking skills and promoting learner-driven methodologies. These are very important areas for experimentation as jobs are increasingly

---

[9]   Jay Mathews, 'Montessori, now 100, goes mainstream', *Washington Post*, 2 January 2007: B1, www.washingtonpost.com/wp-dyn/content/article/2007/01/01/AR2007010100742.html.

[10]   John Dewey, *The school and society and the child and the curriculum*, Chicago: University of Chicago Press, 2013. For criticism of the Lab School approach and its relevance to public schooling see Lee Benson, Ira Richard Harkavy and John L. Puckett, *Dewey's dream: Universities and democracies in an age of education reform: Civil society, public schools, and democratic citizenship*, Philadelphia, PA: Temple University Press, 2007 pp31-33

[11]   Carolyn Pope Edwards, 'Three approaches from Europe: Waldorf, Montessori, and Reggio Emilia', *Early Childhood Research & Practice* 4(1) (2002): n1.

[12]   Edwards, 'Three approaches from Europe', n1.

going to be automated, requiring a significant shift in educational approaches.[13]

Providing more innovative forms of cost-effective education that improve access and quality

If we continue building public education systems in the traditional form – big brick buildings, perhaps with a sports ground, with a classroom that contains desks in rows, with a teacher explaining a concept in front of a blackboard – we will fail to achieve high-quality education. It is also increasingly clear that many forms of what we consider to be 'standard' public education requirements are not worth the cost, as they do not significantly increase learning outcomes for students.[14] In a large school voucher experiment in Andhra Pradesh in India, which tracked comparisons in 23% of the population over four years in the province, researchers found that pupils performed only slightly better in private schools but that the average cost per pupil was less than a third of what it cost to educate a child in a public school.[15] This carries significant implications for improving overall cost-effectiveness in education systems.

Finally, there is also the simple reality that public investment alone cannot ensure that we achieve the Sustainable Development Goal 4 to 'ensure inclusive and quality education for all and promote lifelong learning' by 2030. The best case scenario of a public increase in spending still requires contributions by others (particularly international governments and private philanthropy) to reach the levels of investment necessary to achieve this target and assumes a significant – some reports suggest two- or three-fold – increase in local government investment in education. Sustainable Development Goal 17 specifically recognises the role of a diverse range of actors, including civil society and the

---

[13] Some good examples include the Acton Academies in Texas (www.actonacademy. org), the Rocketship Schools in California (www.rsed.org), High Tech High (www.hightechhigh.org) and Wildflower Montessori Schools in Boston (www. wildflowerschools.org).

[14] Paul Glewwe and Karthik Muralidharan, *Improving school education outcomes in developing countries: Evidence, knowledge gaps, and policy implications*, Working Paper 15/001, University of Oxford, Research on Improving Systems of Education (RISE), 2015.

[15] Karthik Muralidharan and Venkatesh Sundararaman, 'The aggregate effect of school choice: evidence from a two-stage experiment in India', *Quarterly Journal of Economics* 130(3) (2015): 1011–66.

private sector, in creating better mechanisms for implementing the 2030 Agenda.[16]

Conclusion

Whatever the landscape of education looks like in the coming decades, it is almost certain that private, non-state actors – from charter schools, to low-cost private schools, to non-profit operators and an increasing variety of public–private partnerships – are likely to play a role, especially in poorer and developing countries.

If the trend towards more private operators can be imagined in the best possible light, then it should aim, first, to address a combination of the most intractable technical challenges in its particular context. Second, it should experiment pedagogically with innovative forms of learning and so move further away from rote instruction, which has been so damaging in certain public education systems. Third, it should try to overcome problematic cultural legacies, such as racist, sexist or classist traditions. Lastly, it should seek new and collaborative channels of investment in education and develop cost-effective education systems. If done successfully, some of the best schools of this type can present a radical, highly ambitious and compelling vision that shifts the paradigm of what kinds of education are possible for which kinds of learners.

Re-imagining education provision – for black learners in South Africa, for girls in Pakistan, for urban learners in Kenya, for immigrant learners in the US and UK – is essential for realising the equal right to education for all children. Public schools were not built with these demographic groups or their needs in mind. Education initiatives at the margins have found ways to empower, innovate and re-imagine existing educational paradigms to better fit the lives and aspirations of those who have been excluded from formal education systems, from disadvantaged groups to poor communities. These systems have the ability to imagine and implement innovative learning strategies where states either lack the vision or the political will or capacity to implement those initiatives. These schools can work imperfectly, particularly because they lack the resources and the power to be broadly inclusive, and are sometimes even exploitative or offer poor-quality education. But their existence is vital to the project of ensuring the availability of meaningful educational opportunities for all. When governments,

[16] See: http://report.educationcommission.org/report/ p 104 and https://sustainabledevelopment.un.org/sdg17.

civil society, policy advisers and other stakeholders consider the role of these entities, it is useful to engage in what they can do for the broader education project: contextualise, innovate, adapt and redefine.

To put it another way, if the goal of public education is to give everyone an equal opportunity to access education, it is often education at the margins that envisions how good, how relevant and how effective that vision for education can be. Once completely new forms of schooling have been imagined, then those exemplars become the rallying call for justice for all learners. What is imagined at the margins has the potential to break ground for the entire system.

Part II
Balancing the right to freedom of religion and culture and the right to education

---

FOUR

Calling the farce on minority schools

Jayna Kothari

Introduction

Over the last decade and a half we have witnessed radical changes in the development of the constitutional right to education in India. Education has moved from being included in the Directive Principles of State Policy, which was to be made justiciable within 10 years,[1] to being held to be a part of the fundamental right to life under Article 21 of the Constitution[2] and finally to being declared a fully fledged separate fundamental right under Article 21A.[3] The constitutional amendment introducing Article 21A led to the enactment of the Right of Children to Free and Compulsory Education Act 2009 (RTE Act) which gave flesh and blood to the constitutional right to equal and quality education for all children between the ages of 6 and 14 years.

These developments have, however, not been without controversy, particularly with regard to the RTE Act's application to private schools. The Indian Supreme Court in *Society for Unaided Schools of Rajasthan v. Union of India*[4] exempted private unaided minority schools from complying with the RTE Act. Two years later, in May 2014, the Supreme Court in *Pramati Educational and Cultural Trust v. Union of India*[5] extended this exemption to include even minority schools that received grants from the state. Together, these two judgments have exempted all minority schools from the requirements of the RTE Act.

In this article, I argue that the consequences of the minority school exemptions from the RTE Act by the Supreme Court have led to the unfortunate result of a large number of private schools falsely

---

[1] Constitution of India 1950, Art. 45.
[2] *Mohini Jain v. State of Karnataka* [1992] 3 SCC 666; *Unnikrishnan v State of Andhra Pradesh* [1993] 1 SCC 645.
[3] Constitution (86th Amendment) Act 2002.
[4] [2012] 6 SCC 1.
[5] [2014] 8 SCC 1.

clamouring for minority status. This is made possible by the ambiguous definition of what constitutes a minority institution and also the lack of clarity as to who is the authority that would declare schools to be minority schools. There is therefore an urgent need to review the definition of what constitutes a minority institution. But even more fundamentally, it is crucial to argue that minority schools should not be exempted from the norms and standards prescribed in the RTE Act that are necessary for quality education.

The first section of this chapter discusses the articulation of the right to education under the Indian Constitution, and the first phase of litigation under the RTE Act. The second section analyses the unwelcome consequences of the minority exemption to the RTE Act and the confusion it has generated over what constitutes a minority institution. In the third section, I argue for a need to review and rethink the definition of minority institutions in the context of the RTE Act. Finally, this chapter concludes with the argument that minority schools should be required to comply with the norms and standards of the RTE Act because such compliance would not in any way violate any rights of minority institutions. On the contrary, exempting minority schools from compliance with these norms and standards would seriously compromise the RTE Act's vision of providing equal access to quality education for all children.

The right to education under the RTE Act and the first phase of litigation

Education under the Indian Constitution was initially only a Directive Principle of State Policy under Article 45 and not a fundamental right.[6] In 2002, the 86th constitutional amendment codified the right to education as a fundamental right through the introduction of Article 21A in the Indian Constitution.[7] Article 21A casts an obligation on the state to provide free and compulsory education to all children in the age group of 6–14 years.

Though Article 21A was inserted into the Constitution in 2002, it was only in 2009 that the RTE Act was enacted to provide a statutory

[6]   Constitution of India 1950, Art. 45: 'Provision for free and compulsory education for children; – The State shall endeavor to provide, within a period of ten years from the commencement of the Constitution, for free and compulsory education for all children until they complete the age of fourteen years.'

[7]   Constitution (86th Amendment) Act 2002, Art. 21A: 'The State shall provide free and compulsory education to all children of the age of six to fourteen years in such manner as the State may, by law, determine.'

framework for the realisation of the right to quality elementary education. The RTE Act guarantees to every child between the age group of 6–14 years, free and compulsory quality elementary education and obligates the state to satisfy that right. The Act regulates schools and provides for norms and standards that all schools are required to meet.[8] These include requirements on student–teacher ratio, libraries, toilets, midday meals, playgrounds and drinking water. The RTE Act also prohibits corporal punishment, does not allow for children to be held back in a class until the completion of elementary education in the eighth grade and prohibits any sort of screening procedure for admissions. Further, the Act requires teachers and schools to adopt child-centric approaches to learning in a trauma-free context, and conduct continuous and comprehensive evaluation of the child.[9]

One of the most discussed and controversial provisions of the RTE Act has been Section 12(1) (c). This provision mandates that unaided private schools must fill 25% of their student strength in Class I with children from weaker and disadvantaged sections of society, free of cost.[10] The schools would be compensated by the government at the state's cost per child.[11] It was up to the different state governments to provide definitions as to what constitutes weaker and disadvantaged sections of society. Most state government definitions include income criteria so as to ensure that children from poor backgrounds are included and children from scheduled castes, scheduled tribes, migrant families, and children of single mothers, children with disabilities and other disadvantaged sections of society are afforded a place in private schools free of cost. The core reason for this provision in the RTE Act was to foster diversity in schools and to eliminate segregation and discrimination.[12]

With the enactment of the RTE Act, there was the beginning of what I call the first phase of RTE litigation, that is, the large number of constitutional challenges to the Act. The constitutionality of the RTE Act was first challenged by the managements of several private schools in the Supreme Court in *Society for Unaided Private Schools of Rajasthan*

---

[8]   Right of Children to Free and Compulsory Education Act 2009, s 28 (RTE Act).
[9]   RTE Act 2009, s 29.
[10] RTE Act 2009, s 12(1)(c): 'The schools specified in sub-clauses (iii) and (iv) of Clause (n) of Section 2, shall admit in class I, to the extent of at least twenty-five per cent of the strength of that class, children belonging to weaker sections and disadvantaged groups in the neighborhood and provide free and compulsory elementary education till its completion.'
[11] RTE Act 2009, s 12(2).
[12] RTE Act 2009, Statement of Objects and Reasons.

v. Union of India and Others.[13] The core challenge was to the mandate in Section 12 (1)(c) that all aided and unaided private schools fill 25% of their student strength in Grade 1 with children from economically weaker sections and disadvantaged groups. Unaided private schools claimed that such an obligation imposed an unreasonable restriction on their fundamental freedom to practise any trade or occupation under Article 19(1) (g), particularly when they were not getting any funds from the state. They further argued that the state was trying to impose its burden of providing free and compulsory education to private schools. Religious and linguistic minority schools that were unaided also claimed that it violated their special fundamental rights under Articles 29 and 30 of the Constitution to establish and run minority educational institutions.

The Supreme Court in the landmark *Society* judgment in April 2012 upheld the constitutionality of the RTE Act and the principle of horizontal application of social rights to the private sector, but with a significant exception. It held that the Act did not apply to religious and linguistic minority schools that did not get any aid from the state, as the requirement to admit 25% of their student strength from children from disadvantaged groups interfered with their right to establish and administer their own educational institutions under Articles 29 and 30 of the Constitution. This was a huge setback as it excluded private unaided minority schools from its coverage.

Two years after the *Society* judgment, in *Pramati Educational and Cultural Trust v. Union of India & Ors.*,[14] there was a second constitutional challenge to the RTE Act where private school managements argued that the RTE Act made an unjustified distinction between minority and non-minority private schools. The Supreme Court in *Pramati* again upheld the constitutionality of the RTE Act and carved out yet another exception. The Court held that both aided and unaided minority schools were excluded from the purview of the RTE Act as the rights under Articles 29 and 30 applied to all religious and linguistic minority educational institutions. The rationale of the Court in excluding minority educational institutions from the purview of the Act was that the Constitution gives religious and linguistic minorities the fundamental right to establish and administer their own educational institutions, subject only to minimal regulation by the state. Requiring minority schools, aided or unaided, to admit a certain percentage of their students from a specified group was seen as interfering with this

---

[13] *Society for Unaided Private Schools of Rajasthan v. Union of India* [2012] 6 SCC 1.
[14] *Pramati Educational & Cultural Trust v Union of India* [2014] 8 SCC 1.

fundamental right, as it had the potential to undermine the minority character of these institutions.

After four years, there is now yet another petition in the Supreme Court in *Independent Schools Federation of India v. Union of India and Ors*, where the exemption of minority schools from the purview of the RTE Act has been challenged.[15]

The second phase of RTE litigation: the clamour for minority status

Following the *Society* and *Pramati* judgments, all minority schools, both aided and unaided, were exempted from the coverage of the RTE Act, thus greatly diluting the applicability of the RTE Act.[16] A direct consequence of this dilution has been that private aided and unaided schools all over the country began desperately clamouring for minority status so that they can be exempt from coverage under the RTE Act. For example, in October 2014, only a few months after the *Pramati* judgment, the Maharashtra State Child Rights Commission made a startling observation that nearly 80% of private schools in the state had acquired minority status.[17] In Karnataka, there are presently 969 aided and unaided private schools that have been given minority status on linguistic grounds[18] and many more are in the pipeline claiming to be minorities.

Post *Society* and *Pramati*, we started witnessing the second phase of RTE litigation, which consists of private schools filing writ petitions in high courts against state and central government authorities for either compelling them to admit children under Section 12 (1) (c) and the schools refusing to comply based on their self-proclaimed minority status, or litigation challenging government orders where their request for minority status was rejected. This was litigation by private schools

---

[15] WC No. 340 / 2016.

[16] See, for example, Alok Prasanna Kumar, 'Right to education: neither free nor compulsory', *The Hindu*, 19 May 2014, www.thehindu.com/todays-paper/tp-opinion/right-to-education-neither-free-nor-compulsory/article5991271.ece; Anurag Behar, 'Two judgments in education', *Mint*, 14 May 2014, www.livemint.com/Opinion/VLnX9VhIoiq93vRnNkOL6L/Two-judgments-in-education.html.

[17] Vinamrata Borwankar, 'Maharashtra Child Rights Commission seeks to cancel exemption for minority schools', *Times of India*, 16 October 2014.

[18] Department for Public Instructions, Government of Karnataka, *Minority primary schools, teachers and pupils statistics*, www.schooleducation.kar.nic.in/minoedn/MinStatistics/SchTrsPupStat.pdf.

solely to ensure that they do not have to comply with any provisions of a law designed to provide universal and quality education for children. We have witnessed such desperate measures by private schools to declare themselves as minority institutions that, in some cases, some of the private schools had even forged these so-called 'minority certificates' from various government authorities, claiming in court that they are minority schools.[19]

In other cases when litigation was filed by children for being denied admission into private schools on the ground that they are minority schools and high courts directed the schools to admit them, the private schools appealed to the Supreme Court and obtained stay orders.[20]

What is a minority institution and who is the competent authority?

This clamour for minority status and the ensuing litigation by private schools that *Society* and *Pramati* have led to are at least in part a reflection of there being no clear or uniform definition of what constitutes a minority school. Articles 29 and 30 of the Constitution guarantee to religious and linguistic minorities the right to establish and administer

---

[19] 'Bengaluru schools dodging the RTE quota', *The Hindu*, 17 July 2016, www.thehindu.com/news/cities/bangalore/dodging-the-rte-quota/article8737797.ece.

[20] *Karthik Rao and Ors v State of Karnataka & Ors* [2015] WP 29061/2014 (Kar HC) was a petition filed by 50 first grade children, challenging the refusal of five private schools to admit them under Section 12(1) (c) on the ground that they were minority schools. The High Court also directed the schools to immediately admit the children to their respective schools and even pay for their additional classes for the days that they had missed. The appeal to the Supreme Court was in *VIBGYOR School, N S Palya and Ors v. State of Karnataka &Ors* [2015] SC Civil Appeal 10292/2014.

educational institutions.[21] The Constitution, however, does not provide any guidance on what constitutes a religious or linguistic minority institution.

While the Supreme Court has not given a precise definition, it has in a series of judgments provided some guidelines on the characteristics that an institution must possess in order to claim minority status. The Supreme Court's judgments with respect to defining a minority institution refer broadly to three main criteria:

- whether a particular group can claim religious or linguistic minority status should be decided state-wise and not nationally;
- the institution needs to have been established and managed by the minority community; and
- a significant proportion of the school's student body should be comprised of students from that minority community.

The first criterion, of deciding a minority community state-wise, is relatively straightforward. The other two, however, are more complicated.

In *Azeez Basha v. Union of India*,[22] a five judge bench of the Supreme Court held that the expression 'establish and administer' used in Article 30(1) was to be read conjunctively – that the institution should be established by a minority community and that its administration

---

[21] Constitution of India 1950, Art. 29: 'Protection of interests of minorities: (1) Any section of the citizens residing in the territory of India or any part thereof having a distinct language, script or culture of its own shall have the right to conserve the same; (2) No citizen shall be denied admission into any educational institution maintained by the State or receiving aid out of State funds on grounds only of religion, race, caste, language or any of them; 30. Right of minorities to establish and administer educational institutions; (1) All minorities, whether based on religion or language, shall have the right to establish and administer educational institutions of their choice; (1A) In making any law providing for the compulsory acquisition of any property of an educational institution established and administered by a minority, referred to in clause (1), the State shall ensure that the amount fixed by or determined under such law for the acquisition of such property is such as would not restrict or abrogate the right guaranteed under that clause; (2) The state shall not, in granting aid to educational institutions, discriminate against any educational institution on the ground that it is under the management of a minority, whether based on religion or language.

[22] [1968] AIR 662 (SC).

was also vested in that community.[23] Similarly in *St. Stephen's College v. University of Delhi*,[24] the Court pointed out that the onus lay on the minority community to produce satisfactory evidence that the institution in question was indeed established by the minority community claiming to administer it.[25]

More importantly, it was not enough that the institution was merely established or set up by a minority community, but it must also have been established for the 'benefit' of the minority community. In *Andhra Pradesh Christian Medical Association v. Government of Andhra Pradesh*, the Supreme Court held that the government, the university and ultimately the Court may go behind the claim that the institution in question is a minority institution and 'investigate and satisfy itself whether the claim is well founded or ill founded'.[26] The Court pointed out that the purpose of Article 30(1) was not to allow 'bogies to be raised by pretenders but to give minorities a sense of security and a feeling of confidence ... to establish and administer educational institutions of their choice. These institutions must be educational institutions of the minorities in truth and reality and not mere masked phantoms.' The Court held that, 'there must exist some real positive index to enable the institution to be identified as an educational institution of the minorities'.[27]

The final criterion of the Supreme Court, that a significant portion of the student body must be comprised of students from that minority

23 Along similar lines, in *S.P. Mittal v. Union of India* [1983] 1 SCR 729, the Supreme Court held that in order to claim the benefit of Article 30(1), the community must show: (a) that it is a religious/linguistic minority, and (b) that the institution was established by it. Without specifying these two conditions, a community could not claim the guaranteed rights to administer it.

24 [1992] 1 SCC 558.

25 This principle was also reiterated by the Division Bench of the Madras High Court in *T.K.V.T.S.S. Medical Educational and Charitable Trust v State of Tamil Nadu* [2002] AIR 42 (Mad), that 'once it is established that the institution has been established by a linguistic minority, and is administered by that minority, that would be sufficient for claiming the fundamental right guaranteed under Article 30(1) of the Constitution'.

26 *Andhra Pradesh Christian Medical Association v. Government of Andhra Pradesh* [1986] AIR 1490 [SC]

27 The same position had been reiterated in *State of Kerala v. Mother Provincial* [1970] AIR 2079 (SC). In this case, the Supreme Court clarified that the members of the minority community who may establish a minority institution may be a society or trust consisting of members of the minority community, or even a single member of the minority community. What was important, the Court stated, was that 'the intention in either case must be to found an institution for the benefit of a minority community by a member of that community'.

community has led to much controversy as it leads to the inevitable question of what proportion would be appropriate. *In Re Kerala Education Bill,*[28] the Supreme Court held that a minority educational institution may admit a 'sprinkling' of students from non-minority communities without losing its minority character.[29] This concept was further clarified in *P.A. Inamdar v. State of Maharashtra,*[30] which perhaps provides the most detailed reasoning on the subject. In *P.A. Inamdar* the Supreme Court held that:

> minority institutions are free to admit students of their own choice including students of non-minority community and also members of their own community from other States, both to a limited extent only and not in a manner and to such an extent that their minority educational status is lost. If they do so, they lose the protection of Article 30(1) of the Constitution.

The crux of the reasoning in *P.A. Inamdar* is that the minority educational institution is one that is primarily for the benefit of the minority community and that therefore a substantive section of the student population in a minority educational institution should belong to the particular religious or linguistic minority. It has not prescribed what this percentage should be on the basis that this may vary depending on the circumstances.[31]

The broad principles laid down by the Supreme Court in the cases discussed above have given states significant latitude in interpreting the criteria for a minority school. Further, it is worth noting that all of these cases related to institutions of higher education, especially institutions of technical education, and were not in the context of elementary schools under the RTE Act.

---

[28]   [1958] AIR 956 (SC).

[29]   [1958] AIR 956 (SC), para. 40.

[30]   [2005] 6 SCC 537.

[31]   In *T.M.A. Pai Foundation v. State of Karnataka* [2003] AIR 355 (SC) para. 151, the Court observed that: 'It will be more appropriate that, depending upon the level of the institution, whether it be a primary or secondary or high school or a college, professional or otherwise, and on the population and education needs of the area in which the institution is to be located, the State properly balances the interests of all by providing for such percentage of students of the minority community to be admitted, so as to adequately serve the interest of the community for which the institution was established.'

Based on the Supreme Court's guidelines as well as other criteria, states have come up with vastly different definitions of what constitutes a minority school. Some states such as Andhra Pradesh,[32] Haryana[33] and Karnataka have criteria based on both management composition and student strength, though the minimum proportion of students from the minority community varies from 70% in Andhra Pradesh to 25% in Karnataka. In Karnataka, the percentage of student strength of the minority community was actually reduced from 75% in 2012 to just 25% in 2014, under pressure from private schools who were unable to fill up a large percentage of their student strength with members of the minority community.[34] Other states, such as Rajasthan, do not have any requirement for student strength, while the West Bengal criteria simply state that 'as many seats as possible' shall be filled by students from the eligible minority community.[35]

In addition to the confusion over what exactly constitutes a minority school, private schools have also taken advantage of the confusion prevailing as to who is the competent authority to provide them with a minority certificate. While there are state governments issuing minority certificates, certifying schools as minority institutions under the RTE Act, there is also other legislation known as the National Commission for Minority Educational Institutions Act, 2004 (NCMEI Act), under which the 'competent authority' has the powers to grant permission to establish a minority educational institution.[36] The thrust of the arguments of private schools in the second phase of RTE litigation

---

[32] Department of Minorities Welfare, Government of Andhra Pradesh, *Guidelines for issuing minority status certificates in minority educational institutions* (GO 2004/1, 2015), www.aponline.gov.in/Quick%20Links/Departments/Minorities%20Welfare/Govt-Gos-Acts/2004/GO.Ms.1.2004.html.

[33] Director Secondary Education, Government of Haryana, *Guidelines for grant of NOC for minority status* (2015), http://schooleducationharyana.gov.in/downloads_pdf/Circullers/NoticePS_14082015.PDF.

[34] Karnataka State Government, Higher Education Department (Order 2014, GO 2014/1216).

[35] Minority Affairs and Madrasah Education Department Government of West Bengal, *Guidelines for recognition of educational institution as minority educational institution in West Bengal* (GO 2008/942-MD, 2008) www.wbpublibnet.gov.in/form-details/Minorities_Affairs_and_Madrasah_Education-forms/Form%20Of%20Application%20For%20Minority%20Status%20Certificate.pdf

[36] National Commission for Minority Educational Institutions Act 2004, s 10: 'Right to establish a Minority Educational Institution — (1) Subject to the provisions contained in any other law for the time being in force, any person, who desires to establish a Minority Educational Institution, may apply to the competent authority for the grant of no objection certificate for the said purpose.'

is that the state governments cannot lay down a definition as to what constitutes a minority school, and it is only the 'competent authority' under the NCMEI Act which has the powers to do so. These questions are pending adjudication before several high courts all over the country and it is unlikely that we will see a resolution any time soon.

The need for clearer criteria for minority schools

After *Society* and *Pramati*, the consequence of being a minority school is to be exempt from a law that provides a statutory framework for realising the fundamental right to education. Given the widespread repercussions this exemption has had on the implementation of the fundamental right to education, it is of critical importance that the definition of a minority school is clear and narrow to ensure that schools do not proclaim themselves minority schools purely to escape the provisions of the RTE Act.

What should these criteria for a minority school be? As discussed, the Supreme Court in its decisions pertaining to institutions of higher education has proclaimed that whether a particular community is a minority community warranting protection under Articles 29 and 30 of the Constitution should be determined state-wise. The Court further provided that an institution needs to be both established and administered by the minority community in question and that it should primarily cater to the needs of students from that minority community. This meant that while there could be a 'sprinkling of students from non-minority communities', a large proportion of the students should be from the minority community. While these guidelines provide a useful starting point, as we have seen, they have been interpreted by states in very different ways to the detriment of the implementation of the RTE Act. Further, the cases decided by the Supreme Court all pertain to higher education and there may be several reasons to apply slightly different criteria for minority schools.

First, student composition appears to be the most misinterpreted prong of the test. Some states have even done away with the requirement for a minimum percentage of students to be from the minority community altogether, while others have lowered the threshold. This is inconsistent with Supreme Court guidance, which only allows a 'sprinkling' of students from the non-minority community in a minority institution. However, as the Court has also said that what constitutes a reasonable number depends on the circumstances, states have taken a liberal interpretation of the student composition requirement. One argument that has been advanced for not requiring a student composition test or requiring a very small percentage of students to be from the minority community in question is that the minority community may constitute a very small proportion of the population of the state. This was the same argument used by the Government of Karnataka in reducing the required percentage of minority students in a minority school from 75% to 25%.

However, drawing a correlation between the percentage of a minority population in an area and the ability of a school to meet the requirement of enrolling a minimum percentage (e.g. 50%) of minority students in the school involves a logical leap of faith. While any minority community's population, by definition, will be less than 50% in the particular area, this does not translate to a lack of students to meet the state government's requirement in absolute numbers. Even prior to student composition becoming a focus following the *Pramati* judgment, numerous schools run by members of Christian religious minority communities had at least half of their student body belonging to the Christian community. This has been the case despite the fact that Christians constitute less than 5% of the population in most states. On the other hand, lowering the requirement to below 50%, or not having any requirement at all, leads to the risk of schools claiming to be minority schools even though they do not cater to the needs or advancement of the community for whose benefit they claim to be established.

The other prong of the test for a minority institution is that the institution needs to have been both established and administered by members (or a member) of for the benefit of the minority community. The 'established and administered' prong alone should be insufficient to meet this part of the test without evidence of some nexus between the school and the interests of the minority community for whose benefit the school has been established. In *Andhra Pradesh Christian Medical Association v. State of Andhra Pradesh,*[37] the Court spoke of the need for a 'real positive index' that made it clear that the institution in question was for the benefit of the minority community. This sentiment was echoed in *P.A. Inamdar*, where again the Court pointed out that it must always be remembered that the primary purpose of the minority institution was the benefit and protection of the minority community in question.

The aftermath of the *Pramati* decision has led to several schools claiming to be minority schools even though there appears to be no

---

[37] *Andhra Pradesh Christian Medical Association v. Government of Andhra Pradesh and Another* [1986] 2 SCR 749.

correlation between the school and the community that it purports to benefit. Many of these are elite private schools established by a trustee or management who just happen to be from a linguistic minority community. However, apart from the identity of the persons in the management committee, there is no nexus between the school itself and the language or culture of the linguistic minority community, and often these schools do not even teach the language of the linguistic minority community whose interests they say they seek to advance.

Thus, we need clear guidelines and criteria on what constitutes a minority school. As discussed above and in light of the type of abuse by private schools that we have seen, such guidelines must necessarily include a fixed minimum percentage of students from the minority community to be at least 50% of the student strength as well as some evidence as to how the school aims to protect and benefit the interests of the minority community for whom it has been established.

Conclusion

While I would recommend that there should be a clear definition of minority schools, which includes criteria such as 50% of children from the minority community and that the school is actually working for the benefit of the community, they should also comply with the norms and standards prescribed under the RTE Act.

The *Society* and *Pramati* judgments have exempted minority schools not just from Section 12(1) (c), but also from the other provisions of the RTE Act including norms and standards that are applicable to all schools, including requirements for the student–teacher ratio, libraries, separate toilets for boys and girls, midday meals, playgrounds and clean drinking water.[38] The RTE Act also prohibits corporal punishment,[39] does not allow for children to be held back in a class until the completion of elementary education in the eighth grade[40] and prohibits any sort of screening procedure for admissions.[41] One of the glaring errors made by the Supreme Court in both the *Society* and *Pramati* judgments was that while the Court focused on the RTE Act only through the narrow lens of Section 12(1) (c), it ended up providing a broad and blanket exemption for minority institutions from all provisions of the RTE Act and not just from Section 12 (1) (c).

[38] RTE Act 2009, s 19 and Schedule.
[39] RTE Act 2009, s 17.
[40] RTE Act 2009, s 16.
[41] RTE Act 2009, s 13.

There is a strong case for requiring minority schools to comply with these other provisions of the RTE Act and, in particular, the norms and standards in the act, that are the ingredients for a quality education. Even if, for argument's sake, we accept that Section 12(1)(c) may destroy the minority character of an institution, it is entirely unclear how these other provisions of the RTE Act would destroy the minority character of a school or infringe upon the rights of a minority institution under Article 30.[42] On the contrary, we argue that if the state is to fulfil its mandate of ensuring that all children, including children studying in minority schools, obtain a quality education, it is essential that minority schools are also required to comply with the norms and standards.

[42] Constitution of India 1950, Art. 30.

FIVE

The challenge of Afrikaans language rights in South African education

Michael Bishop[1]

Introduction

International human rights law affords linguistic minorities the right to education in the language of their choice. It is an important right, both because home language education is generally more effective, and because educational institutions are vital for maintaining minority communities. South Africa too guarantees a (limited) right to education in the language of one's choice.[2] But for one particular minority community, the Afrikaners, the protection of that right is complicated by South Africa's history of racial inequality, particularly in the area of education. As Moseneke DCJ has put it:

> It is so that white public schools were hugely better resourced than black schools. They were lavishly treated by the apartheid government. It is also true that they served and were shored up by relatively affluent white communities. On the other hand, formerly black public schools have been and by and large remain scantily resourced. They were deliberately funded stingily by the apartheid government. Also, they served in the main and were supported by relatively deprived black communities. That is why perhaps the most abiding and debilitating legacy of our past is an

---

[1]   In this article, I discuss litigation concerning Stellenbosch University. I advised Stellenbosch University on amendments to its language policy, and assisted in an advisory capacity in defending litigation brought against that amended policy. The views expressed in this chapter are mine alone, and not necessarily the views of Stellenbosch University.

[2]   Constitution s 29(2) which I reproduce in full below.

unequal distribution of skills and competencies acquired through education.[3]

As a result of this history of inequality, Black learners today receive, on average, a substantially lower quality of education than their White counterparts. This manifests in the nature of the infrastructure, the learner-to-teacher ratios and the quality of teachers. White children go to schools with excellent facilities and low numbers of students to well-trained teachers. Black children experience the opposite.

In this chapter, I explore how the unique South African context affects the way that we evaluate the right to own-language education of the White Afrikaans minority. I argue that it is not possible to apply the ordinary principles concerning minority languages to Afrikaans. But that does not mean that Afrikaners are not entitled to some protection for their language. Rather, it requires looking for compromises and innovative solutions that acknowledge both the position of privilege built on a history of racial discrimination, and the legitimate demand for protecting Afrikaans-language education.

The argument is structured in three parts. The next section expands on the nature of the problem and how it has manifested in some recent events. The following one looks at the Constitution and how it attempts to mediate between the competing demands. The third section offers some preliminary thoughts on the questions that should frame how the state, the Afrikaans community, courts, schools and universities should tackle the problem.

The nature of the problem

International human rights law creates a clear obligation on states to provide education to minorities in their own language. The Explanatory Note to the Hague Recommendations Regarding the Education Rights

---

[3]   *Head of Department: Mpumalanga Department of Education and Another v Hoërskool Ermelo and Another* [2009] ZACC 32; 2010 (2) SA 415 (CC); 2010 (3) BCLR 177 (CC), at para. 46.

of National Minorities explains that several international instruments[4] 'declare the right of minorities to maintain their collective identity through the medium of their mother tongue. This right is exercised, above all, through education.'[5] The recommendations go on to note that the right to maintain a collective identity must be balanced with 'the responsibility to integrate and participate in the wider national society.'[6]

Under international law, it is understandable that this right is focused primarily on discrimination against minorities who have been historically discriminated against and are denied access to education in their own language. That is the position of most minorities in the world. It is not the position of the White Afrikaans minority[7] in South Africa.

The White minority reaped the benefits of Apartheid by exploiting the Black population. The problem with Afrikaners relying uncritically on the standard international law arguments for the protection of minorities' rights to education in their own language is, as Jonathan

---

[4] The Explanatory Note refers to: the UNESCO Convention Against Discrimination in Education, Art. 5; the Document of the Copenhagen Meeting of the Conference on the Human Dimension of the Conference on Security and Cooperation in Europe, para. 34; the UN Declaration on the Rights of Persons Belonging to National or Ethnic, Religious and Linguistic Minorities, Art.4.3 ('States should take appropriate measures so that, wherever possible, persons belonging to minorities may have adequate opportunities to learn their mother tongue or to have instruction in their mother tongue'); and the Framework Convention for the Protection of National Minorities, Art. 14.

[5] Organization for Security and Co-operation in Europe (OSCE), Hague Recommendations Regarding the Education Rights of National Minorities (1996), www.osce.org/hcnm/32180, at 10. Although this is a European document, it refers to both European and international documents.

[6] OSCE, Hague Recommendations, at 10.

[7] Afrikaans is not only – or even primarily – spoken by White people. Of the 6.8 million people who speak Afrikaans as their first language, 3.4 million are Coloured, and only 2.7 million are White. However, the Coloured community is largely concentrated in two provinces – the Western Cape and (to a lesser extent) the Eastern Cape. There are also 602,000 Black Africans for whom Afrikaans is their first language. See Statistics South Africa, *Census 2011: Census in Brief* (2011), www. statssa.gov.za/census/census_2011/census_products/Census_2011_Census_in_ brief.pdf. However, as a result of geographic legacy of Apartheid, White Afrikaans schools and Coloured Afrikaans schools remain largely separate and unequal. I am concerned in this chapter primarily with White Afrikaans schools. Although some similar considerations might apply to Coloured Afrikaans schools, Coloured people too were victims of Apartheid and the logic that demands accommodation from White Afrikaners does not apply to the Coloured community. For ease of reference, when I refer to Afrikaners or the Afrikaans community, I am referring only to the White Afrikaans community.

Jansen has pointed out, 'their singular lack of acknowledgement of history and politics in analyses that far too often betray an underlying logic of racial protection under the guise of minority rights'.[8] The argument for minority language rights by Afrikaans speakers must be evaluated against the following facts:

> The fact that Afrikaans was one of only two official languages for at least half of the previous century – at the expense of other African languages; that Afrikaans might have been a language spoken by a demographic minority (white Afrikaans), but it was also the language of officialdom of a political majority (white South Africans); that Afrikaans still holds powerful negative memories of its role as the ideological vehicle for suppressing Black nationalist aspirations that climaxed in the 1976 Soweto Student Uprising; and that Afrikaans still carries the heavy burden of white nationalist ambition within post-apartheid society.[9]

It is not possible, against the background of South Africa's history and current inequality to treat the Afrikaans minority in the same way as minorities in other countries as they hold a historically and presently privileged, rather than a disadvantaged position. As the Chief Justice recently explained in a challenge by an Afrikaners' rights group to a decision to change street names in Tshwane:

> Our peculiarity as a nation impels us to remember always, that our Constitution and law could never have been meant to facilitate the frustration of real justice and equity through technicalities. The kind of justice that our constitutional dispensation holds out to all our people is substantive justice. This is the kind that does not ignore the overall constitutional vision, the challenges that cry out for a just and equitable solution in particular circumstances and the context within which the issues arose and are steeped.[10]

[8] J. Jansen, 'Race and restitution in education law and policy in South Africa and the United States', in C. Russo, J. Beckmann and J. Jansen (eds), *Equal education opportunities: Comparative perspectives in educational law*, Pretoria: Van Schaik, 2005, pp 284–5.

[9] Jansen, 'Race and restitution in education law and policy', p 285.

[10] *City of Tshwane Metropolitan Municipality v Afriforum and Another* [2016] ZACC 19; 2016 (9) BCLR 1133 (CC) at para. 19.

But that recognition on its own does not answer the difficult question of how they should be treated, or what the state should do to increase the quality of education for all, against the background of privileged access.

The government has taken a number of steps to equalise the quality of education. In addition to the obvious tasks of improving and building more schools, and increasing the number and quality of teachers, these efforts have included revising funding models and admission policies. The funding model for public schools is designed so that the parents of rich, primarily White schools cross-subsidise poorer, predominantly Black schools.[11] The government has also sought to alter schools' admission policies. Rich White schools often seek to limit their class sizes by restricting the number of children they admit. The result is that mainly poor Black children are forced to attend poorer Black schools which have far higher student-to-teacher ratios. The state has sought to alter existing admission policies in order to more equally distribute learners throughout the system.[12]

A third way in which the state has sought to equalise access to education is by altering schools' existing language policies. The vast majority of Black learners wish to learn in English (at least from grade 6), in part because education in their mother tongue is often not available.[13] In some areas there are Afrikaans-only schools that serve a predominantly White community. These Afrikaans schools generally have better facilities and lower learner-to-teacher ratios than the neighbouring English schools serving the Black community. In order to accommodate the Black learners in an area, and to more equally

---

[11]   Schools are divided into five groups based on the socioeconomic status of their parents and likely students. Those schools serving poorer areas receive more money from the government. The schools in the lowest two quintiles do not charge fees. The schools serving the richer areas make up for the reduced subsidies by charging fees, sometimes quite substantial fees. However, no child can be refused admission to the school because they are unable to afford the fees. They are then entitled to apply for an exemption from the obligation to pay fees.

[12]   See, for example, *MEC for Education in Gauteng Province and Other v Governing Body of Rivonia Primary School and Others* [2013] ZACC 34; 2013 (6) SA 582 (CC); 2013 (12) BCLR 1365 (CC)(upholding province's power to interfere with school admissions policies to ensure more equitable distribution of learners, provided it follows the correct procedure); *Federation of Governing Bodies for South African Schools (FEDSAS) v Member of the Executive Council for Education, Gauteng and Another* [2016] ZACC 14; 2016 (4) SA 546 (CC); 2016 (8) BCLR 1050 (CC) (upholding provincial regulations against a challenge by an organisation representing privileged White schools).

[13]   I return in the conclusion to the irony that Black children are not taught in their own home language.

distribute the public educational resources, the government will seek to change the language policy from Afrikaans-only, to either a dual- or parallel-medium English *and* Afrikaans school.

This raises the hackles of many Afrikaners, who perceive the remaining Afrikaans-only schools as vital for maintaining both the Afrikaans language and culture. The fear is that the Anglicisation of Afrikaans schools (and universities) will lead to cultural and linguistic assimilation – or even 'linguistic genocide' as some have put it. Smit argues:

> that as a result of the national trend of Anglicisation of public schools, approximately 65,000 Afrikaans learners are no longer able to receive tuition in their language of choice and are obliged to receive English instruction. A new pattern of Anglicisation of all schools is not in accordance with the transformative design of the Constitution as it thwarts the constitutional imperative to advance indigenous languages.[14]

Two examples – Ermelo and Stellenbosch University – illustrate this deep clash between the state's commitment to equalising access to education, and the Afrikaans community's desire to maintain their existing access to Afrikaans-language education. Ermelo[15] is a small town in Mpumalanga, east of Johannesburg. In 2007, Hoërskool Ermelo was an Afrikaans-only high school serving 685 learners, including 34 Black learners. The school had 32 classrooms, making an average of 23 learners per classroom. This was far below the national average of 35 learners per classroom, and the occupation at other high schools in Ermelo, which ranged from 38 to 62 learners in each classroom. In 2007, the Provincial Education Department instructed the school to admit 113 English-speaking learners who could not be accommodated in other schools. The school stated that it would only admit learners who agreed to the Afrikaans-only language policy. The department decided that the school was acting unreasonably in refusing to alter its language policy to accommodate the learners. It withdrew the school's power to determine its language policy, appointed an interim committee to determine a new language policy which would

---

[14] M. Smit, '"Collateral irony" and "insular construction": justifying single-medium schools, equal access and quality education', *South African Journal on Human Rights*, 27 (2011): 398 at 421.

[15] *Head of Department: Mpumalanga Department of Education and Another v Hoërskool Ermelo and Another.*

include English. The school took the government to court to challenge the decision.

Second, Stellenbosch University is an historically Afrikaans university, and one of only two universities that remains primarily Afrikaans. Over the last decade it has gradually introduced more and more lectures in English. In 2016, it offered roughly the same number of classes in English as it does in Afrikaans, which reflects the current make up of its student body. It uses dual-language lectures and real-time interpretation in many classes. Still, some modules were only available in Afrikaans. In 2015, a group of concerned students and staff called Open Stellenbosch pointed out that the university's language policy continued to exclude Black students. Unlike their Afrikaans counterparts – who are generally bilingual – the majority of Black students are only conversant in English (which is usually their second language). The use of dual-language classes therefore excluded them. They demanded that the university change its language policy so that English would be the primary language of instruction, with only a secondary role for Afrikaans. In 2015, the university's Council refused to make any changes to the existing language policy. After the decision, Afriforum – a pro-Afrikaner organisation – contended that Open Stellenbosch 'does not have the best interests of students, language or even human rights at heart, but is rather carrying on a vendetta against Afrikaans and Afrikaans speakers'.[16] Open Stellenbosch, by contrast, condemned the decision and called for the Council to be dissolved.[17]

These examples demonstrate the conflict between competing rights and values. On the one hand there is a demand for racial equality and the provision of education to all. That requires drastic changes to the existing educational framework which overwhelmingly favours the White minority. On the other hand, the Constitution is also committed to the protection of minority cultural and linguistic groups, including Afrikaners. That requires (at least for now) the preservation of an inherently unequal system. The next part considers the role the Constitution can play in mediating these tensions.

[16] The statement is at: www.afriforum.co.za/afriforum-applauds-us-councils-decision-victory-language-rights/.
[17] The statement is at: www.politicsweb.co.za/politics/council-must-be-dissolved--open-stellenbosch.

The constitutional position

In this section, I first consider the more general constitutional tension between competing values of diversity and transformation. I then look at the specific rights at issue, before finally focusing on the right in s 29(2) of the Constitution to education in the language of one's choice.

A conflict of values

This specific conflict is part of a deeper friction in the Constitution between what are often mutually supporting values: the commitment to pluralism and diversity, and the guarantee of transformation. In *Pillay* the Constitutional Court held that 'our constitutional project ... not only affirms diversity, but promotes and celebrates it'.[18] Chief Justice Langa continued later: 'our Constitution does not tolerate diversity as a necessary evil, but affirms it as one of the primary treasures of our nation'.[19] That commitment underlies, in part, the right to an education in the language of one's choice in s 29(2). The Constitutional Court has expressly recognised Afrikaans as part of that diversity and supported the need to sustain it as a vibrant language:

> [T]he Afrikaans language is one of the cultural treasures of South African national life, widely spoken and deeply implanted, the vehicle of outstanding literature, the bearer of a rich scientific and legal vocabulary and possibly the most creole or 'rainbow' of all South African tongues. Its protection and development is therefore the concern not only of its speakers but of the whole South African nation. In approaching the question of the future of the Afrikaans language, then, the issue should not be regarded as simply one of satisfying the self-centred wishes, legitimate or otherwise, of a particular group, but as a question of promoting the rich development of an integral part of the

---

[18] *MEC for Education, Kwazulu-Natal, and Others v Pillay* 2008 (1) SA 474 (CC) at para. 65. See also *Minister of Home Affairs v Fourie* 2006 (1) SA 524 (CC) at para. 60.

[19] *MEC for Education, Kwazulu-Natal, and Others v Pillay* 2008, at para. 92.

variegated South African national character contemplated by the Constitution.[20]

At the same time, the Constitution is extremely aware of South Africa's racist past and commits to eradicating it through positive measures to promote those who were previously disadvantaged. Section 9(2) of the Constitution permits affirmative action measures that are 'designed to protect or advance persons, or categories of persons, disadvantaged by unfair discrimination'.[21] The disadvantages of Apartheid are, as noted earlier, particularly prominent in the context of education. In a recent case about affirmative action, the Court held that the Constitution 'has a transformative mission' and is intended to 're-imagine power relations within society' and 'to take active steps to achieve substantive equality, particularly for those who were disadvantaged by past unfair discrimination'.[22] Those active steps could include measures that favour equality at the expense of the rights of the privileged minority.

How, then, does the Constitution weigh the rights of Afrikaans speakers to their language and culture against the rights of Black people to access quality education which was purposefully denied to them for decades?

The rights at issue

The Constitution does not reduce this to a zero-sum game. Instead, it balances the different interests and seeks innovative solutions. It does this through the complex mechanism established by s 29(2). To

---

[20] *In Re Dispute Concerning the Constitutionality of Certain Provisions of the Gauteng School Education Bill of 1995* 1996 (3) SA 165 (CC), at para. 49, quoted with approval in *Head of Department: Mpumalanga Department of Education and Another v Hoërskool Ermelo and Another*, at para. 48.

[21] On the proper interpretation of s 9(2), see *Minister of Finance and Other v Van Heerden* 2004 (6) SA 121 (CC). Importantly, s 9(2) is a defence to a claim of unfair discrimination, if the discrimination meets its requirements. It does not create an obligation on the state to take affirmative action measures.

[22] See, for example, *South African Police Service v Solidarity obo Barnard* 2014 (6) SA 123 (CC) at para. 29 (upholding the refusal to promote a White woman in order to achieve a demographically representative workforce). See also *Solidarity and Others v Department of Correctional Services and Others* [2016] ZACC 18; 2016 (5) SA 594 (CC) (upholding the right to discriminate against a disadvantaged group in order to achieve a representative workforce in the public service, but striking down a plan that relied solely on national demographics without considering regional demographics).

understand how it achieves that end, it is necessary to consider the two sets of rights at play.

On the one hand, the rights supporting the improvement of access to education are threefold:

- First, s 29(1)(a) of the Constitution guarantees a right to a basic education,[23] that is 'immediately realisable'.[24] Section 29(1)(b) grants everyone a right to 'further education', but makes the right subject to progressive realisation and reasonable measures.[25] Both these rights would entitle a student to require the government to take steps to ensure that language is not a barrier to her accessing education.
- Second, s 9(3) of the Constitution guarantees a right not to be unfairly discriminated against on the basis of race or language. If the result of a particular school's language policy – or the combined effect of the language policies of all schools in an area – is that children of one linguistic or racial group have access to inferior education, then they would be able to claim that they have been unfairly discriminated against on the grounds of race or language.
- Third, as noted earlier, s 9(2) permits the state to take measures 'designed to protect or advance persons, or categories of persons, disadvantaged by unfair discrimination'. This affirmative action provision acts as a defence of unfair discrimination against those who had not been subject to historical or ongoing discrimination.[26]

On the other hand, the Afrikaans community can rely on the following constitutional provisions:

---

[23] 'Basic education' includes at least compulsory schooling up to age 15, and probably schooling until the end of high school.

[24] See *Governing Body of the Juma Musjid Primary School & Others v Essay N.O. and Others* 2011 (8) BCLR 761 (CC) at para. 37 ('this right is immediately realisable').

[25] Section 29(1)(b) reads: 'Everyone has the right to further education, which the state, through reasonable measures, must make progressively available and accessible.' Interestingly, unlike the rights to housing, health care, food, water and social security, the right to further education is not expressly subject to 'available resources'.

[26] *Minister of Finance and Other v Van Heerden* 2004 .

- First, the protection of linguistic and cultural rights in ss 30[27] and 31.[28] They guarantee everyone the right to use the language and participate in the cultural life of their choice and to maintain linguistic associations and other organs of civil society.
- Second, s 29(2) grants a limited right to receive education in the language of one's choice. The right exists only when it is 'reasonably practicable' to provide own-language education, and only to a form of education that is reasonable in the circumstances. Section 29(3) grants the right to maintain independent educational institutions, as long as they do not discriminate on the basis of race.[29]
- Third, Afrikaans speakers can also rely on the prohibition against unfair discrimination. They could argue that a decrease in Afrikaans education (that is not a legitimate affirmative action measure in terms of s 9(2)) unfairly discriminates against them on the basis of race or language.

Section 29(2)

The key provision is s 29(2) which seeks to mediate the rights of minority groups with the state's interests in redress and equality. It reads:

> Everyone has the right to receive education in the official language or languages of their choice in public educational institutions where that education is reasonably practicable. In order to ensure the effective access to, and implementation of, this right, the state must consider all reasonable educational alternatives, including single-medium institutions, taking into account –
>
> (a) equity;

[27] Section 30 reads: 'Everyone has the right to use the language and to participate in the cultural life of their choice, but no one exercising these rights may do so in a manner inconsistent with any provision of the Bill of Rights.'

[28] Section 31 reads: '(1) Persons belonging to a cultural, religious or linguistic community may not be denied the right, with other members of that community – (a) to enjoy their culture, practise their religion and use their language; and (b) to form, join and maintain cultural, religious and linguistic associations and other organs of civil society. (2) The rights in subsection (1) may not be exercised in a manner inconsistent with any provision of the Bill of Rights.'

[29] Section 29(3) reads: 'Everyone has the right to establish and maintain, at their own expense, independent educational institutions that – (a) do not discriminate on the basis of race; (b) are registered with the state; and (c) maintain standards that are not inferior to standards at comparable public educational institutions.'

(b) practicability; and

(c) the need to redress the results of past racially discriminatory laws and practices.

To understand s 29(2), it is necessary to focus on three elements: the purpose of the right; the structure of the right; and the negative dimension of the right.

The purpose of the right

The right serves two purposes. It serves to improve access to education as education in one's mother tongue is preferable to education in a different language.

But the right also exists to protect and promote linguistic communities. In the *Gauteng School Education Bill* case, Sachs J said:[30]

> the Afrikaans language, like all languages, is not simply a means of communication and instruction, but a central element of community cohesion and identification for a distinct community in South Africa. We are accordingly dealing not merely with practical issues of pedagogy, but with intangible factors, that ... form an important part of the educational endeavour. In addition, what goes on in schools can have direct implications for the cultural personality and development of groups spreading far beyond the boundary fences of the schools themselves.

This mirrors the position in Canada where the Supreme Court has held: '[e]ducation rights play a fundamental role in promoting and preserving minority language communities. Indeed, "[m]inority language education rights are the means by which the goals of linguistic and cultural preservation are achieved"'.[31] The s 29(2) right is thus intimately linked to the cultural and linguistic rights in ss 30 and 31.

---

[30] In *Re Dispute Concerning the Constitutionality of Certain Provisions of the Gauteng School Education Bill of 1995*, at para. 47.

[31] *Solski (Tutor of) v Quebec (Attorney General)* [2005] 1 SCR 201 at para. 3, quoting *Doucet-Boudreau v Nova Scotia (Minister of Education)* [2003] 3 SCR 3 at para. 26.

The structure of s 29(2)

Section 29(2) consists of 'two distinct but mutually reinforcing parts'.[32] The first part is about whether there is an obligation on the state to provide education in the language of choice. If that hurdle is cleared, the second part determines what form that education should take.

The first part is internally modified by what is 'reasonably practicable'. Adjudicating that standard requires a 'context-sensitive understanding'. In the context of basic education, the Constitutional Court has held that the inquiry demands a consideration of 'all the relevant circumstances of each particular case' including 'the availability of and accessibility to public schools, their enrolment levels, the medium of instruction of the school that its governing body has adopted, the language choices that learners and their parents make, and the curriculum options offered'.[33] Generally, education in the language of choice will be 'reasonably practicable' where a sufficient number of children want education in that language, and no adequate alternative exists.[34]

The Supreme Court of Appeal has explained that, in addition to this 'factual criterion' of logistical possibility, an assessment of reasonableness also requires an assessment of constitutional values: 'The legal standard is reasonableness, which of necessity involves a consideration of constitutional norms, including equity, redress, desegregation and non-racialism.'[35] As I expand on below, it held that the University of the Free State (UFS) had acted reasonably in amending its language policy to virtually abolish Afrikaans tuition where the sole justification for that position was that parallel-medium tuition resulted in a racially segregated campus.

However, s 29(2) does not mean that: 'everyone had the right to receive education in the official language of his or her choice at each and every public educational institution where this was reasonably practicable'.[36] Instead, s 29(2) means:

---

[32] *Head of Department: Mpumalanga Department of Education and Another v Hoërskool Ermelo and Another,* at para. 52.

[33] *Head of Department: Mpumalanga Department of Education and Another v Hoërskool Ermelo and Another,* at para. 52.

[34] S. Woolman and M. Bishop, 'Education', in S. Woolman and M. Bishop (eds) *Constitutional Law of South Africa,* 2nd edn, Cape Town: Juta Legal and Academic, 2007, at 57–9.

[35] *University of the Free State v Afriforum and Another* [2017] ZASCA 32; [2017] 2 All SA 808 (SCA); 2017 (4) SA 283 (SCA) at para. 26.

[36] *Minister of Education, Western Cape, and Others v Governing Body, Mikro Primary School, and Another* 2006 (1) SA 1 (SCA), at para. 30.

everyone has a right to be educated in an official language of his or her choice at a public educational institution to be provided by the State if reasonably practicable, but not the right to be so instructed *at each and every public educational institution* subject only to it being reasonably practicable to do so.[37]

It also means that an individual school or university is not responsible to provide Afrikaans education because other educational institutions have ceased to do so. The obligation to deal with broader patterns rests on the government as a whole, not on individual institutions.[38] Once it is shown that education in the language of choice is reasonably practicable, it is necessary to consider the second part of s 29(2) – the means to fulfil the right.[39] The second sentence of s 29(2) places 'an injunction on the state to consider all reasonable educational alternatives' to achieve the right.[40] In determining what alternatives to employ, 'the state must take into account what is fair, feasible and satisfies the need to remedy the results of past racially discriminatory laws and practices'.[41] Some have argued that s 29(2) creates a preference for single-medium schools over other alternatives.[42] There is nothing in the section to support this reading. Single-medium institutions are mentioned only as an example; the test is equity, practicability and redress. No model has a necessary advantage in meeting those factors. But the combination of factors also means that 'the State cannot simply invoke an overriding commitment to "equality" or "transformation" in order

---

[37] *Minister of Education, Western Cape, and Others v Governing Body, Mikro Primary School, and Another*, at para. 31 (emphasis added).

[38] *Gelyke Kanse and Others v Chairman of the Senate of the Stellenbosch University and Others* [2017] ZAWCHC 119, at para. 94.

[39] Woolman and Bishop, 'Education', p 60.

[40] *Head of Department: Mpumalanga Department of Education and Another v Hoërskool Ermelo and Another*, at para. 53.

[41] *Head of Department: Mpumalanga Department of Education and Another v Hoërskool Ermelo and Another*, at para. 53. The only direct application of the second part of s 29(2) appears in *University of the Free State v Afriforum and Another*, at para. 29, where the Court concluded that English-only tuition was not a reasonable educational alternative. The decision was overturned on appeal, but on the ground that parallel-medium tuition was not reasonably practicable, so the second part of the inquiry was never reached.

[42] See, for example, Smit, '"Collateral irony" and "insular construction"'.

to dismantle single medium institutions.'[43] Single-medium institutions are a legitimate option and the state must weigh up the competing concerns to determine how to meet the right.

The negative dimension of the right

Like all socioeconomic rights, s 29(2) includes both positive and negative aspects. It requires the state to take positive measures to increase access to education in the language of choice, but it also provides a protection against unjustifiable restrictions on existing access to own-language education. As the Constitutional Court held in *Ermelo*: '[W]hen a learner already enjoys the benefit of being taught in an official language of choice the state bears the negative duty not to take away *or diminish the right* without appropriate justification.'[44]

This has important consequences in the context of Afrikaans-language schools. Does changing single-medium Afrikaans schools to dual- or parallel-medium schools diminish the existing access? It seems that conversion to dual medium will diminish access, as part of the teaching will occur in English. Any conversion to dual-medium teaching will therefore require some justification from the state. The obvious advantages of dual-medium teaching for all students may well provide that justification.

A conversion to parallel medium is more complicated. There is no obvious diminishment in the access for the learners, although the additional burden of teaching in both languages could in some instances

---

[43] Woolman and Bishop, 'Education', at p 61. See also *Laerskool Middelburg en 'n Ander v Departementshoof, Mpumalanga Departement van Onderwys, en Andere* 2003 (4) SA 160 (T).

[44] *Head of Department: Mpumalanga Department of Education and Another v Hoërskool Ermelo and Another*, at para. 53. The Supreme Court of Appeal has held that the negative dimension of the right does not create any additional burden. *University of the Free State v Afriforum and Another*, at para. 27. Cachalia JA noted the above statement in *Ermelo*, but then held: 'But this does not mean that once the right exists it continues, regardless of whether the context and the circumstances have changed. A change in circumstances may materially bear on the question whether it is reasonably practicable to continue with a policy. What is required of a decision-maker, when there is a change in circumstances, is to demonstrate that it has good reason to change the policy. In other words, it must act rationally and not arbitrarily.' In short, if the policy is otherwise justifiable in terms of s 29(2), that will be an 'appropriate justification'. The position was supported by the North Gauteng High Court in the litigation concerning the University of Pretoria. *Afriforum and Another v Chairperson of the Council of the University of Pretoria and Others* [2016] ZAGPPHC 1030; [2017] 1 All SA 832 (GP) at para. 54.

reduce the quality of education. The argument against parallel medium (and in part against dual medium) rests primarily on a more general claim: 'Global trends and clear evidence confirms that converting a school to a parallel- or double-medium school inevitably favours the dominant language. This leads to the marginalisation and ultimate extinction of minority non-dominant languages.'[45] The fear is that dual- and parallel-medium schools will gradually result in the complete loss of Afrikaans as a language of learning, and the total Anglicisation of those schools and, ultimately, Afrikaans communities.

The truth of this claim in the specific context of Afrikaans in South Africa is unclear. Afrikaans is the third most spoken language in the country, the second most prominent language for business, and the only language other than English widely used in higher education. Whether widespread conversion to a parallel-medium school will really lead to its extinction is questionable. It is certainly a difficult claim to make in any single instance where the state seeks to alter a school's language policy.

The weaker claim is that a single-medium school better preserves not only instruction in Afrikaans, but the 'ethos' and traditions of the Afrikaans community. This may be true, but it is at most a minor diminution from existing access. But it still engages part of the purpose behind the s 29(2) right.

The argument – in either its strong or weak form – is also a chicken and egg scenario. Does the introduction of English lead to the declined use of Afrikaans? Or does the declining demand for Afrikaans-language instruction (and the increasing demand for English instruction) result in more schools offering both English and Afrikaans? While 61% of Afrikaans single-medium schools have converted to using English in some form, 'many [School Governing Bodies] had voluntarily altered their language policies from Afrikaans single medium to English-Afrikaans parallel or dual medium as a result of diminishing enrolment figures'.[46]

If the claim is false – if the introduction of English will not threaten the existence of Afrikaans – then it is difficult to see why parallel-medium schools do not provide a satisfactory solution. Afrikaans children continue to receive education in their own language, with the additional benefit of the integration that will come from being

---

45 Smit, '"Collateral irony" and "insular construction"', at 416, citing T. Skutnabb-Kangas, *Linguistic Genocide in Education – or Worldwide Diversity and Human Rights?*, Abingdon: Routledge, 2000.

46 Smit, '"Collateral irony" and "insular construction"', at 421.

part of the wider South African community (read: attending a school with a sizeable number of Black children). There is no diminishment of existing access.

However, if it is true that introducing English to existing single-medium Afrikaans schools will decrease access to Afrikaans learning (both at that school and more broadly), and undermine the continued health of Afrikaans culture, then the state will have to justify that change. But proving the truth of that proposition is an evidential burden that those wishing to retain single-medium schools will have to meet. If they are unable to do so, then converting under-used Afrikaans-only schools to parallel medium will not diminish the existing access to the s 29(2) right.

That does not, however, mean that it will necessarily be justifiable to change an existing single-medium Afrikaans school. Even if we are sceptical about the dangers of conversion to dual- or parallel-medium schools, there may be better options to accommodate the learners who wish to learn in English. It may be more appropriate to expand existing English schools, or build new schools, rather than seeking only to accommodate learners who wish to learn in English at existing Afrikaans schools.

There is a final question – when can there be an 'appropriate justification' to abolish access to Afrikaans education altogether by, for example, changing a parallel-medium school to an English-only school, even though it remains 'reasonably practicable' to offer Afrikaans tuition? This question arose in the higher education context in *Afriforum and Another v Chairman of the Council of the University of the Free State and Others*.[47] The UFS had been a parallel-medium English and Afrikaans university. In 2016, it decided to change its language policy to become a single-medium English university (with some minor exceptions). In taking the decision, it did not consider whether it was reasonably practicable to continue to provide Afrikaans tuition. It argued that it was entitled to move to English-only tuition because the consequence of a parallel-medium campus was to entrench racial segregation between the Afrikaans (largely White) group, and the English (largely Black) group. The High Court held that UFS's failure to consider whether it was reasonably practicable – even in light of the claim of segregation – rendered the decision to end Afrikaans classes invalid.

UFS appealed, and the Supreme Court of Appeal (SCA) reversed the High Court's position. As noted earlier, the SCA concluded that the reality that parallel-medium tuition led to de facto racial segregation

[47] [2016] ZAFSHC 130, [2017] 1 All SA 832 (GP).

meant that continued Afrikaans tuition was not 'reasonably practicable', even though it was financially and logistically possible for UFS to continue to teach at least some classes in Afrikaans.[48]

There is some something concerning about the stance adopted by UFS, and endorsed by the SCA. Parallel medium is often the best way to use existing resources to accommodate both English and Afrikaans learners. Yet the logic of UFS is that parallel-medium institutions – which will inevitably involve a degree of racial separation – are inherently constitutionally undesirable. While there is certainly a disadvantage to the separation caused by parallel-medium schools and universities, it must surely be an option contemplated by the second sentence of s 29(2) which requires the consideration of 'all reasonable educational alternatives'. The strong position taken by the SCA seems to rule it out completely – or at least afford schools, universities and the state the option to abandon parallel medium without any further justification. That will make the achievement of the s 29(2) right meaningless in many contexts. It is also likely to result in more absolute segregation as Afrikaans students will seek to move to (private) Afrikaans universities. UFS may succeed in ending separation on its campus, only by promoting greater segregation in the higher education sector as a whole.

The SCA appears to have been aware of this broader systemic problem. It noted that the case raised 'potentially difficult constitutional questions' concerning unfair discrimination against linguistic and cultural minorities, the promotion of 'majoritarian hegemony at the expense of linguistic and cultural diversity' and the undermining of 'the fundamental language scheme of our constitutional order, which requires the State to take practical and positive measures to elevate the status and advance the use of all official languages, instead of diminishing their importance'.[49] But it held that those questions had to be addressed 'through a substantive constitutional challenge to the State's language policy', not by attacking individual universities' policies.[50]

---

[48] *University of the Free State v Afriforum and Another.* The decision was appealed to the Constitutional Court.

[49] *University of the Free State v Afriforum and Another*, at para. 31.

[50] *University of the Free State v Afriforum and Another*, at para. 32. In the recent litigation concerning the University of Stellenbosch, this was interpreted to mean a challenge to the national government's Language Policy on Higher Education, which sets the parameters within which individual universities can adopt their language policies. *Gelyke Kanse and Others v Chairman of the Senate of the Stellenbosch University and Others*, at para. 65.

These conflicts are often framed – as they were in the UFS case – as a winner-takes-all question. Either Afrikaans is kept at its current level or it is abolished entirely. Either we promote transformation or we embrace diversity. This approach is mistaken. In the next section, I argue that the Constitution envisages alternative and innovative ways of resolving these problems that balance all the interests at stake.

Finding resolution

While s 29(2) creates the legal framework within which the Afrikaans community's concerns must be addressed, it requires each demand for own-language education to be evaluated individually. It is not possible to consider all the factors that will be relevant in any individual case. Instead, in this section I consider three issues that repeatedly arise when s 29(2) comes into play.

Schools v state

Perhaps the most important issue is the split responsibility for governing South Africa's schools. The South African Schools Act[51] establishes School Governing Bodies (SGBs) that are given the primary task of running schools. The SGBs are made up of parents and teachers. The SGBs were intended to promote grassroots autonomy and accountability for the management of public schools. The reality is that SGBs at well-resourced schools are highly functional and independent, while those at poorer schools are often dysfunctional.

The SGBs are subject to the general control of the Provincial Education Department (PED) that is responsible for ensuring all children receive an education. The PED can, in some instances, interfere with or take over the powers granted to the SGBs. Virtually all the litigation around school access has involved a conflict between the SGB (attempting to limit access) and a PED (attempting to open access). The SGBs have often been successful, not by defending the substance of their language or admission policy, but by demonstrating that the PED lacked the power to interfere with the decision, or followed the wrong process.[52]

---

[51]   Act 84 of 1996.
[52]   See, for example, *Head of Department: Mpumalanga Department of Education and Another v Hoërskool Ermelo and Another* and *MEC for Education in Gauteng Province and Other v Governing Body of Rivonia Primary School and Others.*

The technical conflict between SGBs and PEDs is likely to continue, although one hopes that PEDs will learn the limits of their powers and act in accordance with them. The Schools Act does generally allow the PEDs to interfere with both language and admission policies, provided it follows the proper processes. If that happens, the debates that reach the courts will likely be more focused on the substantive legitimacy of the SGB's conduct, rather than the procedural legitimacy of the PED's actions. That in fact occurred, most recently, when a group of SGBs took the Gauteng government to court to challenge regulations they claimed interfered with their power to determine admissions policies. In that case, the PED had acted procedurally correctly and the Constitutional Court upheld the substance of its regulations that were designed to enhance equitable access to schools.[53]

There is now a similar potential conflict in the higher education sector. All three universities that have reduced or ended Afrikaans tuition have successfully defended their individual language policies in court. But those courts have also noted some concern about the pattern of reducing Afrikaans tuition and suggested that the national government may need to take a hand. It could well be that, while each individual university acts reasonably, the overall result of rapidly diminishing access to Afrikaans higher education is constitutionally indefensible.

The cause of the problem

This conflict between SGBs and PEDs is linked to an argument that the need to convert the language policies of Afrikaans-only schools is not a symptom of the schools' refusal to change their policy, but of the government's failure to plan properly for increasing enrolment numbers. If the government built or expanded enough English schools to accommodate those students who wished to be taught in English, it would not need to co-opt the resources of Afrikaans schools. The PED, so the argument goes, cannot rely on its failures to justify limiting the language rights of Afrikaners. The same argument can be made in the higher education context – if the government provided greater support to universities that teach in Afrikaans, they would not be under pressure to stop.

There is some truth to this complaint. The cases often arise not as the result of a long-term planning process, but because, at the beginning

---

[53] *Federation of Governing Bodies for South African Schools (FEDSAS) v Member of the Executive Council for Education, Gauteng and Another.*

of a school year, the PED finds that it is unable to accommodate all the learners who wish to attend school; that must be (at least in part) because it has not planned adequately for the future. The longer the current government remains in power, the more difficult it becomes to blame that position on the inequities of Apartheid.

But, at the same time, Black learners should not have to suffer the consequences of the government's incompetence, and Afrikaans learners should not unfairly benefit. When – as was the case in Ermelo – there are children in need of classrooms, and there are classrooms standing empty at an Afrikaans school, the requirements of equity and the right to an education will surely trump the limited interest that Afrikaners have in maintaining single-medium schools. Similarly, when White Afrikaans university students can learn in English, but their Black counterparts cannot speak a word of Afrikaans – as is the case at Stellenbosch – the Constitution endorses a solution that recognises that understanding a lecture at all is more important than being taught in a language of preference.

Yet this type of governance by emergency should not be allowed to become the norm. Afrikaans schools and universities are entitled to demand an approach that considers the legitimacy of their language policy as part of a general strategic plan for schooling in the area. The extent to which the state has a coherent plan for increasing access will be an important factor in assessing whether and how they are justified in changing a particular school's language policy.

Private Afrikaans education

One answer to the problem is for the Afrikaans community – which generally has the necessary resources – to educate their children in independent institutions as they are entitled to do in terms of s 29(3) of the Constitution.[54] This resolution has pros and cons. On the pro side, it allows Afrikaners to continue to educate their children at Afrikaans-only schools (and maybe, in the future, universities), while allowing public resources to be more equitably distributed. If Afrikaans learners leave public schools and universities, those buildings and (some) teachers will be available to teach in English.

But there are two major disadvantages. One, if it is adopted on a wide scale, a large portion of the Afrikaans community will leave the public

---

[54] This suggestion is largely supported by B. Fleisch and S. Woolman, 'On the constitutionality of single-medium public schools', *South African Journal of Human Rights*, 23 (2007): 34.

school system. That will result in continued isolation of the Afrikaans community, rather than integration into the broader South African community. As noted earlier, that is contrary to the goals of integrating minority communities, and contrary to the government's own goals to use the education system to build a more cohesive society.[55] It also demonstrates the irony of arguing for integration as a reason to cease teaching in Afrikaans at public universities – the likely result is more integration on campus, but less integration in the country as a whole.

It will also take out of the public education system the significant amount of money that Afrikaans speakers currently contribute to it. Afrikaans schools remain better than those that serve the Black population because they are subsidised by, often quite large, school fees. If that money is taken to the private school system, it can no longer be used to cross-subsidise education by allowing the state to pay greater subsidies to poor, Black schools. The state will either have to devote additional funds to make up for the shortfall, or lose out on the additional educational resources those funds provide. The possibility of private, Afrikaans-only education is an unattractive and, at most, partial solution to the problem.

Innovative solutions

Instead of seeing the problem as one where either the school or the government wins, it may often be possible to find appropriate compromises that achieve both goals. The two examples I mentioned earlier – Ermelo and Stellenbosch – are instructive.

The Ermelo SGB was ultimately successful in overturning the decision to change its language policy. But it won on technical grounds about how the power had been exercised. The Constitutional Court still ordered the SGB to reconsider its language policy in light of the judgment. It did so, and adopted a policy that moved it to a parallel-medium school, but with an important proviso: the school would first accommodate all Afrikaans learners, the remaining places would then be available for English learners. The solution 'ensures that the Afrikaans learners will not lose their right to public education in a language of their choice, while at the same time enabling learners that cannot be otherwise accommodated, to attend this public school'.[56]

---

[55] See S. Woolman and B. Fleisch, 'The problem of the "other" language', *Constitutional Court Review*, 5 (2014): 135.

[56] Smit, '"Collateral irony" and "insular construction"', at 432.

Unlike UFS (and the University of Pretoria, and the University of South Africa), Stellenbosch University has not ended Afrikaans tuition in order to accommodate English speakers. In 2016 it adopted a new language policy that ensures that no Black student will be excluded because they cannot understand Afrikaans. However, in doing so it sought to avoid any necessary reduction in its Afrikaans offering. It changed the rules of dual-medium lectures to ensure that all information is provided in English, introduced additional real-time translation, and increased the number of parallel-medium lectures. Any reduction in Afrikaans flowing from the implementation of the new policy would occur only to the extent it was reasonably necessary to ensure that no student was excluded. That policy was recently upheld by the High Court.[57]

These instances demonstrate how it can be possible to make existing Afrikaans educational institutions more accessible, and the education system more equitable, without abandoning the good that those schools and universities offer for Afrikaans speakers, and for the country as a whole.

Conclusion

The great 'collateral irony', of course, is that the issue is reduced to a debate between English and Afrikaans, whereas the majority of South Africans use one of the other nine official languages as their home language. The reason, as Moseneke DCJ explained, is that '[l]earners whose mother tongue is not English but rather one of our indigenous languages, together with their parents, have made a choice to be taught in a language other than their mother tongue'.[58] The education system acknowledges this by teaching in mother tongue in the early years, before gradually moving to education in either English or Afrikaans as the language of instruction in later years. While it is easy to understand the benefit of fluency in English – it is the primary South African

---

[57] In September 2016, an Afrikaans non-governmental organisation – Gelyke Kanse (Equal Chances) – launched a review of the new language policy. It relied on alleged violations of Afrikaans students's 29(2), 29(1)(b) and s 9(3) rights, as well as a violation of s 6 of the Constitution. On 25 October 2017, shortly before this chapter was finalised, the Western Cape High Court delivered a judgment dismissing the application. See *Gelyke Kanse and Others v Chairman of the Senate of the Stellenbosch University and Others*. The judgment is currently the subject of an appeal in the Constitutional Court.

[58] *Head of Department: Mpumalanga Department of Education and Another v Hoërskool Ermelo and Another*, at para. 49.

language of government and business, and one of the global languages – it is harder to understand why Afrikaans should be used as a medium of instruction throughout the schooling and university system, while Sepedi, Sesotho, Setswana, siSwati, Tshivenda, Xitsonga, isiNdebele, isiXhosa and isiZulu are not. The only reason is one tied up with South Africa's racist history – the Apartheid state invested heavily in Afrikaans as an academic language, and forced people to teach and learn in Afrikaans. While government policy encourages a similar investment in the other nine official languages, it has (understandably) not been forthcoming on nearly the same scale. Moreover, as Afrikaans is used less and less as a language of business and administration (outside certain regions), the disparity between it and the other African languages is increasingly difficult to justify.

But that does not justify the 'equality of the graveyard' where Afrikaans schools must be abolished because no other minority language has its own schools. Rather it suggests that the government should be investing in more mother-tongue schools for all language groups. Still, 'as the state and everyone else is well aware, the national purse, the resources of individual schools, the availability of appropriately trained teachers and the adequacy of existing textbooks across all 11 official languages place cognisable, constitutionally-recognised limits on our capacity to deliver immediately upon this laudable goal'.[59] It is not possible to immediately create schools and universities for all the South African languages. Deciding what to do with the existing Afrikaans institutions in a way that balances the rights of Afrikaners with the demands for more equitable education for all races and languages is a difficult and important question for South African education and constitutional law. It should be resolved in a way that attempts, as far as possible, to recognise and promote all the legitimate interests at stake.

Postscript

After this chapter had already been sent to proofs, the Constitutional Court handed down its decision in *AfriForum and Another v University of the Free State*.[60] The decision refuses leave to appeal against the judgment of the Supreme Court of Appeal in *University of the Free State v Afriforum and Another* which is discussed above. The Constitutional Court did not grant a hearing in the matter.

The Constitutional Court largely confirmed the analysis of the Supreme Court of Appeal, over the dissent of Froneman J (Cameron

---

[59] Woolman and Fleisch, 'The problem of the "other" language', at 142.
[60] [2017] ZACC 48; 2018 (2) SA 185 (CC).

J concurring). The judgment – written by the Chief Justice – also resonates with the basic theme of this chapter – the need for careful solutions to difficult problems. The Chief Justice recognised that: 'Issues around language policy are as emotive as the language itself. This would be especially so where plans are afoot to effect changes that would water down the role or usage of language, particularly Afrikaans. For, Afrikaans has for many years been associated with dominion or power.'[61] At the same time, the Chief Justice warned that we 'must consciously guard against the possibility of a subliminal and yet effectively prejudicial disposition towards Afrikaans setting in, owing only to its past record as a virtual synonym to "racism and racially based practices".'[62] Recognising these deep constitutional and emotional tensions, Mogoeng CJ wrote: 'It is a difficult transformational issue that requires a meticulous and detached handling by all true defenders and ambassadors of our constitutional vision.'[63]

Froneman J – a White Afrikaner – would have set the matter down for a hearing. Clearly contemplating the future of Afrikaans in South Africa, he wrote the concluding part of his judgment in Afrikaans. 'Is all lost for Afrikaans?', he asked, before suggesting how it might be saved.[64] He stressed the need for White Afrikaans speakers to both confront the history of oppression, and seek a new, inclusive future.[65] Tellingly, he criticised the applicant – Afriforum – for the manner in which it had approached both the policy debate in the University, and the litigation:

> [W]hat is singularly lacking in the applicants' founding affidavit is any recognition of the complexity of the language rights of others and the unequal treatment of oppressed people of other races in the past, let alone the continued existence of historic privilege. No practical suggestions were apparently made to accommodate the needs of other race groups and facilitate language instruction during the University's extensive inquiry into the problem. There is no apparent insight into these realities, nor any realisation of the perception that this creates in others. These failures entrench the caricature of Afrikaners as intransigent and

[61] Ibid. at para. 3.
[62] Ibid. at para. 5.
[63] Ibid. at para. 4.
[64] Ibid. at para. 130.
[65] Ibid. at paras. 131-2.

insensitive to the needs of others. The applicants need to ask themselves whether their manner of attempting to protect language rights advances the cause of Afrikaans or hinders it.[66]

That is exactly what I have tried to suggest in this chapter. The future – for both sides of this debate – is in recognising the deep emotions and interests invoked, and seeking to accommodate the other through practical and innovative ways of using scarce educational resources.

[66] Ibid at para. 134.

Part III
Gender equality in education: moving beyond access to primary education

SIX

Women and education: the right to substantive equality

Sandra Fredman

Introduction

In September 2015, the world committed itself to ensure inclusive and equitable quality education and to promote lifelong learning opportunities for all by 2030. At the same time, it promised to achieve gender equality and empower all women and girls within the next 15 years. These ambitious proclamations came at the close of the 15-year period set by the Millennium Development Goals (MDGs) to achieve equality in primary education between boys and girls. Although the United Nations Development Program (UNDP) claims to have achieved that goal, a closer look reveals that there is still a long way to go. It is argued here that the notion of equality as parity, which has been used in measuring the achievements of the development goals, is too limited. Simply treating girls and boys equally will not address the gendered power relations which lead to ongoing inequality in education. Instead, it is argued that the principle of substantive equality should be the framework for evaluating progress towards equality in education. This requires attention to be paid to redressing disadvantage; addressing stigma, stereotyping, prejudice and violence; facilitating participation; and accommodating difference and achieving structural change.

Development goals and human rights

In 2015, the UNDP proudly proclaimed: 'The world has achieved equality in primary education between girls and boys.' Equality in primary education was one of the three targets set in 2000 to be achieved by 2015 as part of the third MDG goal of promoting gender equality and empowering women. However, a closer look at the statistics shows that in fact only 64% of countries in the developing regions had achieved gender parity by 2012. Nor do these statistics give a full picture. Statistics refer to enrolment rather than completion. In fact, the MDG 2015 report states that almost 100 million adolescents are still not completing primary school. More worrying still, there were 57 million out-of-school children of primary school age in 2015.[1] Of these 55% were girls. Moreover, nearly half (48%) of out-of-school girls are unlikely ever to go to school compared to about 37% of out-of-school boys.

The Sustainable Development Goals (SDGs) agreed in 2015 are more ambitious. SDG4 commits the world to ensuring inclusive and equitable quality education and to promote lifelong learning opportunities for all by 2030. Its specific targets include ensuring that all girls and boys complete free, equitable and quality primary and secondary education leading to relevant and effective learning outcomes. It also commits to building and upgrading education facilities that are child, disability and gender sensitive, and to increasing the supply of qualified teachers.

SDG5 is the stand-alone gender equality goal. It aims to achieve gender equality and empower all women and girls. As well as committing to end all forms of discrimination against women and girls everywhere, its targets include the elimination of all forms of violence against all women and girls, and the elimination of all harmful practices, such as child, early and forced marriage, and female genital mutilation. SDG5 also sets specific targets aiming to recognise and value unpaid care and domestic work both through the provision of public services and the promotion of shared responsibility within the household; to ensure women's full and effective participation and equal opportunities for leadership; to ensure universal access to sexual and reproductive health and reproductive rights; to undertake reforms to give women equal rights to economic resources, and to adopt and strengthen sound policies and enforceable legislation for the promotion of gender equality and the empowerment of all women and girls at all levels.[2]

The SDGs need to be read together with the binding human rights commitments which have already been made, both internationally and domestically. There is a widespread commitment to the right to education in the International Covenant on Economic, Social and Cultural Rights (ICESCR).[3] The Covenant has been ratified by 164 countries in the world, with a further 6 who have signed but not ratified

[1]   *The Millennium Development Goals report 2015*, New York: United Nations.
[2]   www.un.org/sustainabledevelopment/gender-equality/.
[3]   ICESCR Article 13.

it.[4] Although the right itself is stated to be progressively realisable subject to maximum available resources,[5] there is an immediate obligation to ensure the equal right of men and women to the enjoyment of the rights in the Covenant, including of course, the right to education.[6] In addition, the Convention on the Elimination of All Forms of Discrimination against Women (CEDAW) has been ratified by 189 countries in the world.[7] CEDAW includes a duty on state parties to ensure women enjoy equal rights with men in the field of education, a right which is elaborated on in some detail, as will be seen below.[8] There are also many domestic instruments which guarantee a right to education and a right to equality for men and women. The South African Constitution gives an immediate right to a basic education, including adult basic education (Section 29), and Section 21A of the Indian Constitution gives the right to 'free and compulsory education to all children of the age of six to fourteen years'. Both constitutions also guarantee equality between men and women.

Unlike the MDGs, the SDGs explicitly refer to human rights. The preamble declares:

> The 17 Sustainable Development Goals and 169 targets which we are announcing today demonstrate the scale and ambition of this new universal Agenda. They seek to build on the Millennium Development Goals and complete what these did not achieve. They seek to realize the human rights of all and to achieve gender equality and the empowerment of all women and girls. They are integrated and indivisible and balance the three dimensions of sustainable development: the economic, social and environmental.

However, it is important to underline the differences between development goals and human rights. Development goals are political commitments, vulnerable to changing priorities. Certainly, wavering political priorities are one reason that some of the MDG goals were not fully achieved. Human rights, by contrast, are legally binding

---

[4]   http://indicators.ohchr.org/ (as of 1 December 2015).
[5]   ICESCR Article 2.
[6]   ICESCR Article 3.
[7]   http://indicators.ohchr.org/ (as of 1 December 2015)
[8]   CEDAW, Article 10. See also the Convention on the Rights of the Child, Article 28.

commitments, both internationally and on individual states. Second, development goals are seen as transfers of aid or even charity. A human rights-based approach characterises individuals as rights bearers, capable of insisting on their rights, rather than as beneficiaries of charity or aid. Third, human rights are universal. The focus of the MDGs was on developing regions, although a major step forward for the SDGs is that they also now apply to developed countries. This is important because even in developed countries there are vast inequalities and pockets of real poverty. Fourth, the success of development goals is measured in aggregate quantitative terms. Hence the claim that the goal of equality in primary education between girls and boys has been achieved. Human rights insist that each individual matters. The fact that there are 55 million out-of-school children means that there are 55 million children whose rights are being breached.

The major outstanding question for the SDG agenda is the means of implementation. The 2030 Agenda for Sustainable Development sees every country as having primary responsibility for its own economic and social development, while at the same time committing to a 'revised Global Partnership'. Overseas Development Aid (ODA) providers reaffirmed their commitments, such as achieving a target of devoting 0.7% of their gross national income to ODA in developing countries.[9] It is argued here that progress should be measured against the standard of substantive equality. States' binding commitments to gender equality and to the right to education require an immediate commitment to eliminating discrimination, so that women and girls can genuinely enjoy their rights, not just to education but also in education and through education. What then does substantive equality entail? It is to this that I now turn.

Substantive equality for women to, in and through education

The limitations of formal equality, or the principle that likes should be treated alike, are by now well-rehearsed.[10] In the context of education, there are several specific limitations. Treating girls and boys alike might mean that equality could be achieved by parity of

---

[9] https://sustainabledevelopment.un.org/post2015/transformingourworld

[10] S. Fredman, *Discrimination law*, 2nd edn, Oxford: Oxford University Press, 2011; S. Fredman, 'Beyond the dichotomy of formal and substantive equality: towards a new definition of equal rights', in I. Boerefijn et al (eds), *Temporary special measures*, Cambridge: Intersentia, 2003.

enrolment, even if many children remain out of school. It might also mean that equality could be achieved by extending education at the cost of diminishing quality, or 'levelling down'. Yet a 2012 OECD report[11] unequivocally shows that 'equity can go hand in hand with quality'.[12] More fundamentally, simply treating girls and boys alike will not address the specifically gendered disadvantage which continues to obstruct girls and women in relation to education.

The right to equality should instead encompass a notion of substantive equality. The meaning of substantive equality remains somewhat contested, with some focusing on dignity, others on equality of opportunity, and still others on equality of results. I have argued that instead of reducing substantive equality to a single principle, it should be regarded as having four interconnected dimensions. First, rather than regarding equality as a symmetric principle, which treats likes alike regardless of antecedent disadvantage, the right to equality should focus on redressing disadvantage. This is the distributive dimension. Second, substantive equality should address stereotyping, prejudice, stigma and violence. This is the recognition dimension. Third, substantive equality should facilitate voice and participation, especially where marginalised groups have little voice in the political process or are excluded socially. This is the participative dimension. Fourth, substantive equality should not assume that everyone should conform to a single dominant norm. Equality does not mean sameness. Instead, substantive equality should embrace difference and aim for structural change, which reconfigures the dominant norm. This is the transformative dimension. These dimensions are not in any lexical order of priority. They buttress each other and also help to address conflicting pressures. For example, where a measure targeted at disadvantage is stigmatic or entrenches stereotyping, it needs to be adjusted accordingly. The application of these dimensions to the right to gender equality in education is elaborated below.

Although this chapter focuses on gender, it should be stressed that it refers to all women and girls, regardless of ethnicity, sexual orientation, disability or ability, religion, age or socioeconomic position. Indeed, when disadvantage is intersectional or cumulative, the need for substantive equality is greater rather than less. It is notable that, despite the global figures indicating improvement in education, the most disadvantaged have seen the least gains. The MDG report

[11] OECD, *Equity and quality in education*, www.oecd.org/education/school/50293148.pdf.

[12] OECD, *Equity and quality in education*, p 3.

from 2014 points out that poverty, gender and living in rural areas are the most pervasive factors linked to disparities in school attendance. Indeed, in sub-Saharan Africa, only 23% of poor, rural girls complete primary education.[13] The OECD report therefore stresses that an equitable education system should redress the effect of broader social and economic inequalities. It should mean both that 'personal or social circumstances such as gender, ethnic origin or family background, are not obstacles to achieving educational potential (fairness) and that that all individuals reach at least a basic minimum level of skills (inclusion)'[14]

Redressing disadvantage: the distributive dimension

The first dimension of substantive equality aims at redressing disadvantage. Redressing disadvantage prevents levelling down. It is not enough simply to achieve parity of enrolment, if this means a reduction in the quality of education. It is also not sufficient if large numbers of girls and boys remain excluded from school. This dimension of substantive equality therefore goes well beyond parity, and requires that the right to quality education must be equally available to all. From a gender perspective, it goes further. It requires note to be taken of the specific forms of disadvantage which impede girls and women from achieving quality education. A focus on redressing disadvantage in this sense therefore requires attention to be paid to the 'underlying determinants' of the right to education, in the same way as the right to health requires attention to be paid to the underlying determinants of health. Applying this to the right to education, it can be seen that the right to education needs to be considered in the context of the many interlocking obstacles to gender equality more broadly.

One clear example is the role of sanitation. Lack of sanitation in schools has a serious effect on children's right to education, leading to illness, lack of privacy and absenteeism. As many as 443 million school days are lost every year due to sanitation and water-related issues.[15] However, it has a specific effect on girl learners, especially when they are menstruating. It has been shown that the lack of adequate sanitary facilities in so many schools contributes to absenteeism and the high rate of drop-out of girls.[16] Girls who have to relieve themselves in the open are also vulnerable to attack or to the fear of attack.

[13]   *The Millennium Development Goals Report 2014*, New York: United Nations, p 17.
[14]   OECD, *Equity and quality in education*, p 9.
[15]   www.unric.org/en/sanitation/27281-sanitation-as-a-human-right.
[16]   www.unicef.org/wash/index_schools.html

But it is not only the lack of water and sanitation in schools themselves that affect girls' ability to access their right to education. It is also the lack of water and sanitation in the home. UNICEF points out that household chores, including fetching water, keep many girls out of school. Without access to water, all household chores become very much more onerous, and since most household chores, including cleaning latrines and garbage disposal, fall to women and girls, this is very likely to interfere with school attendance. Moreover, when family members fall sick, frequently as a result of poor hygiene, girls are more likely to be kept out of school to care for them.[17] Even in schools, girls might be expected to fetch water and clean latrines. Thus a key to boosting girls' attendance at school would be to provide water closer to home, and to ensure that there are safe, clean and private sanitation facilities at school.[18] 'Investing in making access to safe water, sanitation and menstrual hygiene management universal in every school is crucial in ensuring that every girl is granted her human right to education.'[19] This is also a virtuous circle. As UNICEF also shows, schools can be the catalyst for change, through teaching hygiene, providing role models and thereby influencing the hygiene habits of the family and the wider community.

A further specifically gendered disadvantage relates to early childbearing and the resulting missed opportunities for schooling. As discussed in greater detail in 'Equality and Education: Let's Talk About Sex Education' (chapter 7 in this edited collection), several provisions in CEDAW require states parties to take all appropriate measures to give women access to family planning.[20] However, contraception is only available to 26% of women in sub-Saharan Africa. Moreover, in many areas, pregnant learners are still excluded from school, and even if they are de facto permitted, no accommodation is made to facilitate their continued education. The expulsion of pregnant learners has been an issue of growing concern among the human rights community. From her earliest report, the first UN Special Rapporteur on the right to education, Katerina Tomasevski, consistently drew attention to the pervasiveness of the exclusion of pregnant learners from school, highlighting the practice as a breach of the right to education and

---

[17] www.unicef.org/wash/index_schools.html
[18] www.unicef.org/wash/index_schools.html
[19] B. Mengistu, 'Her right to education', WaterAid, March 2013, p.6, http://docplayer.net/10069830-Her-right-to-education-how-water-sanitation-and-hygiene-in-schools-determines-access-to-education-for-girls.html (accessed 12 March 2018).
[20] See Articles 5(b), 10(h) and 16(1)(e) of CEDAW.

non-discrimination.[21] More recently, the Committee on the Rights of the Child, noting the pervasiveness of such practices, made it clear that 'discrimination based on adolescent pregnancy, such as expulsion from schools, should be prohibited, and opportunities for continuous education should be ensured'.[22] This has also been a common refrain on the part of the CEDAW Committee, which on numerous occasions has expressed concern at exclusion of pregnant learners and urged states to ensure that they are able to stay in school.[23] A particularly emphatic declaration by the Supreme Court of Colombia underlined that 'the conversion of pregnancy ... into a ground for punishment violates fundamental rights to equality, privacy, free development of personality and to education'.[24] The practice has not, however, abated. According to a 2014 report by the Centre for Reproductive Rights, mandatory pregnancy testing and expulsion of pregnant school girls continues in a number of African countries including Tanzania, Ghana, Kenya, Nigeria, Sierra Leone, Uganda and Zimbabwe.[25]

Similarly, women's ongoing disadvantage in the workforce is both a result and a cause of inequity in education. While the right to education might be the springboard to greater opportunities in the workforce, the reality of women's limited access to employment, their predominance in precarious and flexible work, and the stubborn persistence of job segregation and the pay gap may deter families from investing in girls' education. In North Africa, women still hold fewer than one in five paid jobs in the non-agricultural sector, a figure which

[21] Economic and Social Council 'Preliminary report of the Special Rapporteur on the right to education, Ms Katarina Tomasevski' (Commission on Human Rights, E/CN.4/1999/49, 13 January 1999). Preliminary report of the Special Rapporteur on the right to education, Ms Katarina Tomaševski, submitted in accordance with Commission on Human Rights Resolution 1998/33, E/CN.4/1999/49, Geneva: Economic and Social Council, 1999.

[22] Committee on the Rights of the Child, General Comment No. 15: The right of the child to the enjoyment of the highest attainable standard of health (Art. 24), 62nd Session, UN Doc. CRC/C/GC/15, 2013, para. 56.

[23] See, e.g., CEDAW Committee, Concluding Observations: Chile, para. 29(a), UN Doc. CEDAW/C/CHL/CO/5-6, 2012; CEDAW Committee, Concluding Observations: Saint Lucia, para. 28, UN Doc. CEDAW/C/LCA/6, 2006.

[24] *Corte Constitucional de Colombia, Crisanto Arcangel Martinez Martinez y Maria Eglina Suarez Robayo v. Collegio Cuidad de Cali*, No. T-177814, 11 November 1998; cited by K. Tomasevski, 'Girls' education through a human rights lens', www.odi.org/sites/odi.org.uk/files/odi-assets/publications-opinion-files/4349.pdf.

[25] Centre for Reproductive Rights, Submission for Half-day of General Discussion and Draft General Recommendation on the Right to Education, 14 June 2014. www.ohchr.org/Documents/Issues/Children/2030/CRR.pdf.

is unchanged since 1990. Sexual harassment, violence in and around school, child marriage and early pregnancy, as well as lack of 'proper toilets and sanitation, disproportionately affect girls, interfering with their education and their future job prospects.[26] There are also serious intergenerational consequences. It has been shown that the mothers' educational level plays a crucial role in both physical and mental development of their children.

The recognition dimension: addressing stigma, stereotyping, prejudice and violence

There are three facets to the recognition dimension of substantive equality which illuminate the specific gendered disadvantage in relation to education. The first is the way in which gender stereotypes can be perpetuated at school. Stereotypes of masculinity and femininity are reinforced in many ways in the school environment, through the curriculum, teacher expectations, and interactions between pupils. This is dealt with specifically as part of the right to education in CEDAW. Under Article 10 of CEDAW, states should take all appropriate measures to ensure:

> the elimination of any stereotyped concept of the roles of men and women at all levels and in all forms of education by encouraging coeducation and other types of education which will help to achieve this aim and, in particular, by the revision of textbooks and school programmes and the adaptation of teaching methods.

Second, the recognition dimension illuminates the ways in which girls and women are locked into reproductive roles. Possibly the most stubborn obstacles to full participation are cultural expectations that women will remain primarily responsible for children and housework. Where such cultural barriers are invested with religious significance, they are even harder to shift. Article 5 CEDAW also addresses this issue. Under Article 5, states should take all appropriate measures to 'ensure that family education includes a proper understanding of maternity as a social function and the recognition of the common responsibility of

---

[26] Human Rights Watch (2016) *The Education Deficit: Failures to Protect and Fulfil the Right to Education in Global Development Agendas* p.49, https://www.hrw.org/report/2016/06/09/education-deficit/failures-protect-and-fulfill-right-education-through-global (accessed 13 March 2018).

men and women in the upbringing and development of their children, it being understood that the interest of the children is the primordial consideration in all cases'.

The third and particularly serious facet is violence, both at school and on the way to and from school. Violence against women is now recognised to have reached pandemic proportions. For example, the Special Rapporteur on violence against women, in her recent visit to South Africa, expressed her dismay and distress at the epic proportions of violence against women in South Africa. It is therefore crucial to link the commitment in SDG5 to eliminating violence against women to the achievement of equity in education. Girls are being violently shut out of schools in many places, whether by the Taliban, Boko Haram, so-called Islamic State or other groups. Attacks on girls and abductions of schoolgirls and female teachers by extremist groups in many part of the world have severely impacted in girls' access to education.[27]

Recent research also shows the extent of violence within schools. Sexual harassment, as well as violence both in school and on the way to school are key obstacles to girls remaining in school or enrolling for secondary education. Girls are especially vulnerable due to unequal power relations and gender stereotypes. Particularly disturbing is the extent of sexual violence by teachers: 16% of children in Togo named a teacher as responsible for the pregnancy of a classmate. This has long-term implications. It sets up violent role models, perpetuating the cycle of violence across generations. It has serious physical consequences, including HIV, STIs and psychological trauma. Not surprisingly, it leads to poor education outcomes for the girls affected. SDG5 goes further and recognises as a form of violence against women all forms of forced marriage, including child marriage. This is a serious obstacle to girls' possibilities of progressing in education.

The participation dimension

The third dimension of substantive equality refers to voice and participation. Education is obviously a key to giving voice to the disadvantaged. At the same time, it is crucial that the educational programmes for girls are able to take into account and integrate the concerns of girls themselves. This is true in relation to the curriculum, the organisation of the school, and gender-based violence. The voices of women teachers should also not be excluded.

[27] Ibid. p.63.

A personal experience of mine was when we were building the case for the right to sanitation in the Eastern Transvaal in South Africa, where many schools had no toilets or toilets which were seriously inadequate. I expected the girl learners I spoke with to tell me that they would not come to school when menstruating because of the lack of toilets. They did not say that though. Instead, they said that access to sanitary towels was the key. When they ran out of sanitary towels, or if they did not have any in the first place, that was when they did not come to school. And when I investigated further, I found that this was a widespread problem. Giving voice to women will allow the design of the SDGs to genuinely further the right to substantive equality and therefore the right of equality for women.[28]

Transformation and structural change

The fourth dimension requires structural change. Schools need to provide a safe environment, proper sanitation, the provision of reproductive health care, and the accommodation of pregnant learners. Curricula need to be changed so that gender equality is facilitated. Some of these changes are not hugely resource intensive. One is the provision of sanitary towels. Here the relative cost compared to the benefits to girls is small.

A key structural change concerns the teaching profession. Good-quality teachers, who are given good terms and conditions and who are also dedicated to their work, is clearly a key necessary structural change. In many parts of the world, the majority of primary teachers are women, and this feminisation of the teaching profession brings with it lower pay and lower status. Paradoxically, though, almost all of the 32 countries where women do not form the majority of primary school teachers are in Africa (although they constitute 79% in South Africa).[29] This might reflect the very fact that women in these countries are not accessing education, as well as the difficulty they have in obtaining decent paid work. Thus, when considering quality of teachers as the key to structural change, it is important to pay attention to the gendered nature of paid employment itself.

[28] Human Rights Watch The Education Deficit (above, note 26), p.54–58.
[29] http://data.worldbank.org/indicator/SE.PRM.TCHR.FE.ZS and see also Alia Wong, 'Let Women Teach', *The Atlantic*, 19 Nov. 2015, www.theatlantic.com/education/archive/2015/11/let-women-teach/416304/.

Conclusion

It has been argued here that the right to equality demands much more than parity for girls and boys in education. Simply requiring parity ignores the specifically gendered way in which inequality in education manifests itself. Instead, a substantive approach to equality requires attention to be paid to redressing disadvantage, addressing stigma, stereotyping, prejudice and violence, facilitating participation and accommodating difference, and achieving structural change. This chapter has briefly sketched some of the issues illuminated by a substantive approach to equality. It is to be hoped that in developing SDG policies, vigilance will be exercised in ensuring a substantive approach to equality, and that human rights and the SDGs can work together to make a real difference to the ways in which the right to equality can be fully enjoyed by girls and women.

SEVEN

Equality and the right to education: let's talk about sex education

Meghan Campbell

Girls face numerous challenges in exercising their right to education. Attendance for girls in secondary and tertiary schools is significantly behind boys.[1] Girls are routinely and often violently prevented from getting to school.[2] However, a focus on access is not sufficient. If a right to education is to be an empowering and multiplier right, it is crucial to examine how the content, structure and delivery of education can perpetuate and reinforce gender inequalities.[3] International human rights law has under-utilised potential for contributing to the realisation of gender equality in education. The Convention on the Elimination of Discrimination Against Women (CEDAW), the prominent legal instrument on women's human rights, includes provisions that ensure rights within and through education.[4] While this chapter focuses on a specific component of education, sex education, it should be placed in context and understood as part of the larger challenge of ensuring that a right to education promotes gender equality.

Sex education is required by all people, including boys and men, and specifically for disabled persons and sexual minorities.[5] Many of the obstacles that limit sex education apply equally to boys, men and disadvantaged groups; however, there is a subset of obstacles that

---

[1] United Nations (UN), *The Millennium Development Goals Report 2015*, New York: UN, p 29, www.un.org/millenniumgoals/2015_MDG_Report/pdf/MDG%20 2015%20rev%20(July%201).pdf.

[2] UN, *The Millennium Development Goals Report 2015*, p 29.

[3] UN Committee on the Elimination of Discrimination Against Women (CEDAW Committee), Concept note on the draft recommendation on girls'/ women's right to education, www.ohchr.org/EN/HRBodies/CEDAW/Pages/ Womensrighttoeducation.aspx, para. 5.1.

[4] Adopted 20 November 1980, entered into force 2 September 1980, 1577 UNTS 3.

[5] Report of the UN Special Rapporteur on the right to education, UN Doc. A/65/162, 2010, para. 87(d).

uniquely engage the gender relations between men and women. The UN Committee on Economic Social and Cultural Rights notes that 'due to women's reproductive capacities', it is essential that girls and women have the information on sexuality and reproduction to make meaningful decisions about their lives.[6] Thus it is imperative to take an asymmetric approach and analyse the connection between sex education and the equality of women and girls. It is argued that the delivery of human rights-based sex education is a positive obligation on the state to fulfil girl's right to equal education and gender equality under CEDAW.

The first section of this chapter analyses the current challenges girls face in accessing human rights-based sex education. Sex education sharply brings into focus the discriminatory gender norms that influence and undermine a girl's right to education and the accountability challenges that are becoming increasingly pervasive throughout all of education. The second section uncovers the relationship between sex education and the state's positive obligation to achieve a right to education. The following section evaluates how the CEDAW Committee has developed this obligation. The final section investigates how the positive obligation to provide sex education can be fully developed so as to ensure that equality in education empowers girls and women.

The obstacles to sex education

Girls and women face a myriad of interwoven challenges in accessing sex education. To address these challenges prominent actors within the UN – the Special Rapporteur on the right to education, the UN Education, Scientific and Cultural Organisation (UNESCO) and the UN Population Fund (UNFPA) are developing standards for sex education. These actors are explicitly calling on states to approach sex education from a human rights perspective. Under this new approach sex education must provide adequate knowledge on reproduction, sexually transmitted infections (STIs), the law on consent to sexual activity, and violence against women. Human rights-based sex education seeks to

---

[6]   UN Committee on Economic, Social and Cultural Rights (CESCR), General Comment No. 22: On the right to sexual and reproductive health, UN Doc E/C.12/2016/22, 2016, para. 25.

transform stereotypical gender norms and relationships and includes a diverse perspective on sex and sexual relationships.[7]

Denmark, Norway, Sweden, Finland and the Netherlands are examples of good practice as sex education is based 'on the premise of young people as "rights-holders"'.[8] Sadly, in many states there is no provision of sex education in schools. In Malawi over half of students aged 15–19 have not received sex education.[9] In many countries in sub-Saharan Africa 'almost half of the people who received sexual education received no information on [key] topics … contraception, pregnancy … [STIs] and the right to say no to sex'.[10] In Ethiopia and Angola there is no provision for sex education.[11]

Rather than breaking cycles of gender inequality, there is evidence that sex education is being used to entrench traditional roles. In certain schools in Poland girls are taught that contraception is a barrier to loving relationships and can cause cancer.[12] In Senegal, family values, marriage, women's roles in caring and reproduction are emphasised in sex education over gender equality.[13] UNFPA notes that some Eastern and Southern African countries have sex education policies that aim 'at instilling fear in adolescents towards sexual and reproductive health'.[14] In the US, sex education programmes rely on stereotypes of women's

---

[7] Report of the UN Special Rapporteur on the right to education, UN Doc. A/65/162, 2010, para. 76, para. 87(d).

[8] Heather D. Boonstra, 'Advancing sexuality education in developing countries: evidence and implications', *Guttmacher Policy Review*, 14(3) (2011).

[9] Report of the UN Special Rapporteur on the right to education, UN Doc. A/65/162, 2010, para. 57.

[10] Report of the UN Special Rapporteur on the right to education, UN Doc. A/65/162, 2010, para. 55.

[11] UNFPA, *Harmonizing the legal environment for adolescent sexual and reproductive rights*, 2017, www.up.ac.za/media/shared/1/ZP_Files/unfpa-esaro-laws-and-policy-review-on-asrhr-2017.zp119762.pdf, p 18.

[12] Susanne Heuck and Jessica Mowles, 'Love your neighbour, but not too much: political and religious involvement in sex education within Polish public school', Humanity in Action, www.humanityinaction.org/knowledgebase/214-love-your-neighbor-but-not-too-much-political-and-religious-involvement-in-sex-education-within-polish-public-schools.

[13] International Planned Parenthood Federation (IPPF), *Over-protected and under-served: A multi-country study on legal barriers to young people's access to sexual and reproductive health: Senegal*, www.ippf.org/sites/default/files/ippf_coram_senegal_report_eng_web.pdf, 2014, p 16.

[14] UNFPA, *Harmonizing the legal environment*, p 18.

dress and behaviour to buttress abstinence-only arguments.[15] One student workbook warns that 'girls need to be aware they may be able to tell when a kiss is leading to something else'.[16] The lack of human rights-based sex education can have disastrous consequences for girls and women. Girls may have very limited knowledge of their rights to be free from violence, to consent to sexual activity, and the right to access and use sexual and reproductive health services.[17] Without sex education there is an increased risk of girls becoming pregnant. In many countries in sub-Saharan Africa girls can be expelled from school or face stigma upon their return to class.[18] Due to a lack of further education, young mothers can become trapped in reproductive roles or are only able to access low-paid, informal and precarious work.[19] This creates a vicious cycle of disadvantage.

There is no single explanation for the obstacles facing girl's access to human rights-based sex education. There are many cross-cutting factors. Two of the most prominent and interconnected are (i) conservative religious and cultural norms; and (ii) the lack of recognition of and accountability for the state's positive obligation to provide sex education. The UN Special Rapporteur on the right to education observes that human rights-based sex education is often 'obstructed in the name of religious ideas'.[20] The 'recognition of customary law in some [Eastern and Southern African] countries creates an impediment to dealing with harmful cultural practices' through human rights-based sex education.[21] For example, in Canada, the Ontario provincial government has unveiled new comprehensive compulsory curriculum for sex education. There has been strong

---

[15] John Delamater, 'Gender equity in formal sexuality education', in Sue Klein et al (eds), *Handbook for achieving gender equity through education*, 2nd edn, Abingdon: Routledge, 2007, p 415.

[16] Delamater, 'Gender equity in formal sexuality education'.

[17] IPPF, *Over-protected and under-served … Senegal*; IPPF, *Over-protected and under-served: A multi-country study on legal barriers to young people's access to sexual and reproductive health: El Salvador*, 2014, www.ippf.org/sites/default/files/ippf_coram_el_salvador_report_eng_web.pdf.

[18] Rebecca Davis, 'Analysis: when schoolgirls fall pregnant, why don't we talk more about rape?', *Daily Maverick*, 23 January 2015, www.dailymaverick.co.za/article/2015-01-23-analysis-when-schoolgirls-fall-pregnant-why-dont-we-talk-more-about-rape/#.VcNXpDbbLIU.

[19] UN Special Rapporteur on the right to education, Report to the Human Rights Commission (Girl's Education), UN Doc. E/CN.4/2004/45, 2004, para. 78.

[20] Report of the UN Special Rapporteur on the right to education, UN Doc. A/65/162, 2010, para. 5.

[21] UNFPA, *Harmonizing the legal environment*, p 15.

opposition to this from parents and faith-based schools arguing that the curriculum 'dismantles biblical perspectives on human sexuality ... by an aggressive agenda of the LGBT [movement]'.[22] There are similar faith-based objections to sex education in Peru, the UK, Senegal and El Salvador.[23]

The influence of conservative sociocultural and religious norms is made possible due to the lack of recognition of the state's positive obligation to provide sex education in both public and private institutions.[24] Often there is no legal framework mandating the content of sex education within the school. In Latin America and the Caribbean nine states have no specific legalisation on sex education and in six European states sex education is not compulsory.[25] Even if national legislation or regulation is in place, it often remains unimplemented or is not properly supported. While there is detailed and comprehensive guidance for sex education in both Northern Ireland and England, it is not a compulsory component of the curriculum and there is little pressure placed on schools to adopt the state's guidelines.[26] At other times, the law gives primacy to religious and cultural norms. In England, the law stipulates that 'due regard to the moral considerations of family life' must be had in the delivery of sex education and parents have the 'absolute right to remove their child from [sex education]'.[27]

CEDAW's commitment to sex education

Given the significant and pressing obstacles girls face, what role can the international human rights law framework, particularly CEDAW, play in ensuring that sex education is based on human rights and furthers gender equality? At first glance, this question may appear redundant as various UN bodies have already developed standards for sex education. Arguing for greater engagement by CEDAW and the

[22] Pete Baklinski, 'Christian private school rejects Wynne's sex-ed as "perverse"', 14 July 2015, www.lifesitenews.com/news/christian-private-school-rejects-wynnes-sex-ed-as-perverse.

[23] IPPF, *Over-protected and under-served ... Senegal*; IPPF, *Over-protected and under-served ... El Salvador*; IPPF, *Over-protected and under-served: a multi-country study on legal barriers to young people's access to sexual and reproductive health: UK*, 2014, www.ippf.org/sites/default/files/ippf_coram_uk_report_web.pdf.

[24] UN Special Rapporteur on the right to education, Report to the Human Rights Commission, para. 37, para. 39.

[25] Report of the UN Special Rapporteur on the right to education, UN Doc. A/65/162, 2010, para. 42.

[26] IPPF, *Over-protected and under-served ... UK*, p 14.

[27] IPPF, *Over-protected and under-served ... UK*, p 14.

CEDAW Committee seemingly places it in competition with other actors in the UN system. However, this position overlooks the multiple ways that CEDAW can enrich and complement the activities of the UN Special Rapporteurs, UNESCO and UNFPA. Crucially, CEDAW and the CEDAW Committee can situate sex education within existing *legal* frameworks and accountability mechanisms. A clear understanding at the international level that human rights require the provisions of sex education can be a catalyst to shift dialogue in the domestic sphere. If a positive obligation to provide sex education is interpreted as being included within CEDAW, it can inspire individuals, civil society, courts and legislators to interpret similarly framed domestic human rights to include sex education.[28] While there is no direct guaranteed route between domestic human rights and CEDAW, there is evidence of the power of the CEDAW framework to influence and shape domestic norms, particularly in the context of gender-based violence.[29] Moreover, CEDAW has its own sophisticated accountability system. Through the periodic reporting process, individual communications and inquiry procedures the CEDAW Committee can constructively engage with the state on sex education and hold it accountable for its commitments.

To achieve these goals it is first necessary to understand how CEDAW requires the state to provide human rights-based sex education that ensures girls and women are able to enjoy their human rights. A careful analysis of the CEDAW demonstrates (i) that there are provisions concerning sex education and (ii) that the commitment to achieve equality in CEDAW places a positive obligation on the state to provide sex education.

A right to sex education

CEDAW contains three explicit obligations on sex education. Article 5(b) requires the state to ensure that '*family education* includes a proper understanding of maternity as a social function and the recognition of the common responsibility of men and women in the upbringing ... of their children'. Article 10(h) of CEDAW requires states to ensure on an equal basis 'access to specific educational information to help

---

[28] See for example, *Vishaka v. State of Rajasthan* (1997) 6 SCC 241 (Indian Supreme Court).

[29] Judith Resnik, 'Comparative (in)equalities: CEDAW, the jurisdiction of gender and the heterogeneity of transnational law production', *International Journal of Constitutional Law*, 10(2) (2012): 531, 542.

ensure the health and well-being of families, including information and advice on *family planning*'. And, finally, Article 16(1)(e) of CEDAW guarantees that women have 'the same rights to decide freely and responsibly on the number and spacing of their children and have access to the information, *education* and means to enable them to exercise these rights'. Combined, these provisions 'speak to the importance of providing a base from which decisions about family size and other health related issues can be made'.[30] This gives the CEDAW Committee the legal basis to review the state's sex education policies and programmes.

A right to gender equality

Although there are direct provisions on sex education, for pragmatic reasons it is helpful to understand how CEDAW's commitment to gender equality includes a positive obligation to provide sex education. One of the aims of the CEDAW and the international human rights framework is to positively influence the development of domestic human rights. Most jurisdictions do not recognise a right to sex education or family planning as contained in Articles 5(b), 10(h) and 16(1)(e). Thus, recognising the connection between gender equality and sex education ensures that individuals, domestic grassroots and civil society organisations can use the right to equality, which is protected in a majority of domestic human rights instruments, to argue for sex education.

The role of equality in CEDAW

The first step is to understand how equality is defined and framed in CEDAW. There is no free-standing right to equality in the treaty. Instead states are required to take all appropriate measures to eliminate discrimination against women in various fields and achieve gender equality.[31] For example, Article 10 of CEDAW, 'states shall take all appropriate measures to eliminate discrimination against women in order to ensure them *equal* rights ... in the field of education'. Equality is the goal of eliminating discrimination against women and

---

[30] Fareda Banda, 'Article 10', in Marsha A. Freeman, Christine Chinkin and Beate Rudolf (eds), *CEDAW: A commentary*, Oxford: Oxford University Press, 2013, p 269.

[31] CEDAW Committee, General Comment No. 28: Of core obligations under Article 2 of CEDAW, UN Doc. CEDAW/C/GC/28, 2010.

is at the heart of the state's legal obligations under CEDAW. Rights to employment, health, participation in public life, economic and social life and equality for rural women are all similarly framed.

Somewhat surprisingly, CEDAW does not define equality and the CEDAW Committee has not articulated a definitive meaning. It is clear that equality in CEDAW is multifaceted and contains both formal and substantive equality. The CEDAW Committee explains that formal equality is identical treatment between men and women.[32] But to achieve true equality, it is crucial to move towards substantive equality. The CEDAW Committee has not articulated a coherent understanding of substantive equality. At times it indicates substantive equality requires: differential treatment;[33] an equal start; 'an enabling environment to achieve equality of results';[34] 'strategies for overcoming underrepresentation of women and a redistribution of resources and power between men and women';[35] 'the ability to develop personal ability ... [to] make choices without the limitation set by stereotypes, rigid gender roles and prejudices';[36] and 'real transformation of opportunities, institutions and systems so that they are no longer grounded in historically determined male paradigms of power and life patterns'.[37]

This definition of substantive equality hints at a further model of equality: transformative gender equality. The CEDAW Committee has not yet explicitly stated that CEDAW is premised on transformative gender equality, but it tends 'to view transformative equality as part of substantive equality rather than as a distinct model of equality'.[38] The academic literature consistently holds that this model of equality is included in CEDAW.[39] Fredman's influential model of transformative

---

[32] CEDAW Committee, General Recommendation No. 25: Temporary special measures, UN Doc. CEDAW/C/GC/24, 2004, para. 8.

[33] CEDAW Committee, General Recommendation No. 28, para. 16.

[34] CEDAW Committee, General Recommendation No. 25, para. 8.

[35] CEDAW Committee, General Recommendation No. 25, para. 8.

[36] CEDAW Committee, General Recommendation No. 28, para. 22.

[37] CEDAW Committee, General Recommendation No. 25, para. 9.

[38] Simone Cusack and Lisa Pusey, 'CEDAW and the rights to equality and non-discrimination', *Melbourne Journal of International Law*, 14 (2013): 54, 63.

[39] Cusack and Pusey, 'CEDAW and the rights to equality and non-discrimination', 54, 63; Andrew Byrnes, 'Article 1', in Freeman et al (eds), *CEDAW: A commentary*, 56.

equality is prominent in the text of CEDAW.[40] This model of equality pursues four overlapping aims: breaking the cycle of disadvantage; promoting respect for dignity and worth; accommodating difference by achieving structural change and promoting political and social inclusion; and participation. The CEDAW Committee's comments, referred to above, on transforming institutions and stereotypical gender norms, indicates that it implicitly understands that equality within CEDAW is transformative.

The relationship between gender equality and sex education

Applying the different models of equality in CEDAW demonstrates the important role of sex education in furthering girls' and women's equality. Formal equality would require the removal of any de jure restrictions on girls and women accessing sex education. For example, if the school only provided sex education to boys but not to girls.

In respect to substantive and transformative equality, it is helpful to apply Fredman's four-dimensional model of equality as this framework is, in practice, being used by the CEDAW Committee and other UN human rights treaty bodies.[41] The first element, breaking the cycle of disadvantage recognises that individuals and groups have suffered because of their personal characteristics and to redress this imbalance positive measures are required. Due to biological and sociocultural factors, girls and women are in significant need of sex education. The most prominent example is in relation to pregnancy and childbirth. Complications 'during pregnancy and childbirth is the second largest cause of death for 15–19 year old girls globally'.[42] It is estimated that 22 million unsafe abortions are performed each year.[43] Adolescent pregnancies are more likely in poor, uneducated and rural communities because 'some girls do not know how to avoid getting pregnant: sex education is lacking in many countries'.[44] To prevent maternal

---

[40] Sandra Fredman, *Discrimination law*, Oxford: Clarendon Press, 2011, chapter 1; Meghan Campbell, 'Women's rights and the Convention on the Elimination of Discrimination Against Women: unlocking the potential of the optional protocol', *Nordic Journal of Human Rights*, 34(4) (2016): 247.

[41] Sandra Fredman and Beth Goldblatt, *Gender equality and human rights*, Discussion paper for Progress of the World's Women 2015–2016, UN Women, 2015.

[42] WHO, 'Fact Sheet No. 364: Adolescent pregnancy', September 2014, www.who.int/mediacentre/factsheets/fs364/en/.

[43] WHO, 'Fact Sheet No. 388: Preventing unsafe abortion', July 2015, www.who.int/mediacentre/factsheets/fs388/en/.

[44] WHO, 'Fact Sheet No. 364: Adolescent pregnancy'.

mortality and morbidity, and to realise gender equality for poor, rural girls the state must take positive measures to ensure that sex education is taught in all classrooms and, most specifically, in the overlooked and marginalised classrooms where poor, rural girls go to school. A new phenomenon where girls and women are disadvantaged is cyber-safety. With the advent of technology there is a rise in girls and women sharing sexually explicitly images and videos of themselves.[45] Girls and women who make these images can be socially shamed, humiliated, bullied, harassed and threatened.[46] The law has been very slow to respond to the harms of sexting,[47] making sex education on these issues of particular importance for girl and women.

The dignity element addresses recognition of harms, including harassment, prejudice and violence. Cultural norms valorise boys and men as powerful sexual agents and praise male promiscuity, while female sexuality is restricted, passive and 'seen as shameful and degrading'.[48] Girls and women feel stigmatised in expressing their sexuality[49] and using sexual and reproductive health services.[50] Women are held responsible for any unintended consequences of sexual activity and for the reproduction and caring of children.[51] As mentioned above, in some countries girls are expelled from school on becoming pregnant. Sex education can be a powerful tool to dismantle these norms and 'encourage rethinking of traditional roles'.[52]

Turning to gender-based violence, while there is broad recognition that violence against women is systemic, pervasive and entrenched, 'this has not led to the adoption of coherent and sustainable' remedial

[45] Victoria Law Reform, 'Inquiry into sexting', Parliamentary Paper No. 230, Session 2010–2013, 2013: 21, 41.

[46] Canadian Paediatric Society, 'Sexting: keeping teens safe and responsible in a technically savvy world', Feb. 2014, www.cps.ca/documents/position/sexting.

[47] Laura Hilly, 'UK efforts to criminalize revenge porn: not a scandal, but a sex crime', OxHRH Blog, 31 October 2014, http://humanrights.dev3.oneltd.eu/uk-efforts-to-criminalize-revenge-porn-not-a-scandal-but-a-sex-crime/.

[48] IPPF, *Over-protected and under-served ... El Salvador*, p 22.

[49] Victoria Law Reform, 'Inquiry into sexting'.

[50] IPPF, *Over-protected and under-served ... El Salvador*, p 12; IPPF, *Over-protected and under-served ... Senegal*, pp 10–13. See also, Inga Winkler and Virginia Roaf, 'Bringing the bloody dirty linen out of the closet: menstrual hygiene as a priority for achieving gender equality', *Cardozo Journal of the Law and Gender*, 21 (2015): 1.

[51] IPPF, *Over-protected and under-served ... Senegal*, pp 16–19; IPPF, *Over-protected and under-served ... UK*, 35–8.

[52] Report of the UN Special Rapporteur on the right to education, UN Doc. A/65/162, para. 63.

strategy.[53] The UN Special Rapporteur on violence against women recommends that states 'engage in transformative remedies' that empower and build women's capacities to 'facilitate the questioning of hegemony within cultures'.[54] Sex education can emphasise girls' and women's right to bodily integrity and autonomy, teach the laws on sexual consent, link gender-based violence to human rights and encourage young men and women to critically reflect on gender relations. It is an important transformative measure in a larger strategy to end gender-based violence and achieve gender equality.

The third element, the structural element, ensures that institutions accommodate difference. The state must ensure that sex education programmes are properly supported through adequate funding, monitoring and teacher training. To valorise diversity, sex education should positively portray different types of sexual relationships.

Finally, participation requires the state to meaningfully consult with women and girls. The participation element is the most challenging as women and girls can have diverse understandings on the role of sex education in furthering gender equality. These challenges are considered in greater depth in the section 'Strengthening sex education in CEDAW'. Here it is only necessary to note that a commitment to gender equality requires the participation of all women and girls, even the most marginalised and oppressed in the design and delivery of sex education.

Uncovering the relationship between sex education and gender equality engages the substantive obligations in CEDAW. Sex education is a crucial preventive strategy to protect women and girls from maternal mortality and morbidity stemming from unwanted pregnancies (equality in health care, Article 12); it can challenge entrenched gender norms on sexuality and caring roles (cultural attitudes, Article 5); it provides the necessary information and critical thinking skills (education, Article 10) to empower girls and women to protect their bodily integrity (family life, Article 16) and achieve economic independence (employment, Article 11, and economic and social life, Article 13). Sex education is a facet of gender equality and thus to achieve equality in public and private life, the state must provide human rights-based sex education.

---

[53] UN Special Rapporteur on violence against women, Report to the Human Rights Council (Twenty Years), UN Doc. A/HRC/26/38, 2014 para. 57.
[54] UN Special Rapporteur on violence against women, Report to the Human Rights Council, para. 60.

The CEDAW Committee's approach to sex education

The CEDAW Committee is using its accountability mechanism to draw attention to the relationship between gender equality, women's human rights and sex education. The CEDAW Committee takes a holistic approach calling on states to provide sex education to fulfil women's rights to equality in education, health and family life. It holds that sex education should be a mandatory part of the curricula and addresses gender equality, violence, prevention of STIs, reproductive and sexual health rights, gender relations and harmful practices.[55] It further stresses that sex education should pay specific attention to the needs of girls, seek to empower girls to make responsible sexual choices, reduce teen pregnancy and guarantee women's bodily autonomy.[56] Its recommendations to Argentina are a good example of the CEDAW Committee's approach. It encourages the state to:

> Ensure the implementation of Law 26.150 of 2006 that creates the National Comprehensive Sex Education Programme across all provinces and its incorporation in the regular school curriculum, as well as the training of teachers to deliver the programme in an age appropriate manner at all levels of education, aimed at promoting responsible sexual behaviour and preventing adolescent pregnancy and sexually transmitted diseases[57]

Under the Optional Protocol to CEDAW, the CEDAW Committee has held states accountable under Article 10(h) (family planning) and Article 16(1)(e) (number of children) of CEDAW for failing to provide information on birth control, although this has been in the context of health care rather than sex education.[58]

[55] CEDAW Committee, Concluding Observations: Spain, UN Doc. CEDAW/C/ESP/CO/7-8, 2015, paras. 26–27; CEDAW Committee and Committee on the Convention on the Rights of the Child, General Recommendation No. 31: On harmful practices, UN Doc. CEDAW/C/GC/31, 2014, para. 68.

[56] CEDAW Committee, General Recommendation No. 19: On violence against women, UN Doc. CEDAW/C/GC/19, 1992; CEDAW Committee, General Recommendation No. 28: Of core obligations, para. 21; CEDAW Committee, Concluding Observations: St Vincent's and Grenadines, UN Doc. CEDAW/C/VCT/4-8, 2015, para. 29(b).

[57] CEDAW Committee, Concluding Observations: Argentina, UN Doc. CEDAW/C/ARG/7, 2016, para. 29(a).

[58] *A.S. v Hungary*, CEDAW/C/36/D/4/2004; CEDAW Committee, Prohibitions on contraception in the Philippines, UN Doc. CEDAW/C/OP.8./PHL/1, 2015.

There is a growing awareness on the part of the CEDAW Committee that there is an obligation in CEDAW to provide sex education. There are concerns as to how consistent the CEDAW Committee is when discussing sex education. In the periodic reporting round for November 2016, the CEDAW Committee only raised sex education as a concern in three out of eleven Concluding Observations.[59] However, even more problematic the CEDAW Committee is not addressing the key obstacles to realising human rights–based sex education in the classroom. First, as discussed in the first section, 'Obstacles to sex education', there is no reference to conservative religious and cultural norms that oppose the strengthening of human rights–based sex education in the classroom. Without explicitly addressing this, the CEDAW Committee is missing out on making recommendations that tackle the de facto challenges to sex education. As a result, their recommendations are at risk of being ignored or perceived as irrelevant. Second, the CEDAW Committee is not consistently addressing the legal mechanisms and accountability structures that the state needs to put in place to fully realise a positive obligation for sex education.

Strengthening sex education in CEDAW

CEDAW is beginning to recognise the transformative potential of sex education. It is necessary to take the next step forward and ensure that the CEDAW Committee's recommendations address the de facto challenges to realising sex education. This final section explores the legal arguments to address these challenges and proposes how the CEDAW Committee's recommendations can be modified so as to tackle the obstacles to sex education.

The role of religion and culture

Arguably the biggest obstacle to recognising a positive obligation to provide human rights–based sex education is opposition from conservative religious and cultural groups. These groups argue that it is against their religious and cultural norms to have information on sex education in the classroom. They campaign either to have sex

---

[59] CEDAW Committee, Concluding Observations: Argentina, UN Doc. CEDAW/C/ARG/7, 2016, para. 29(a); CEDAW Committee, Concluding Observations: Canada, UN Doc. CEDAW/C/CAN/CO/8-9, 2016, para. 37(b); CEDAW Committee, Concluding Observations: Honduras, UN Doc. CEDAW/C/HND/CO/7-8, 2016, para. 33(d).

education removed from the classroom, or to limit its content or to have individual or institutional faith or moral-based exemptions.

CEDAW is a strong advocate for women and in the past the CEDAW Committee has been sceptical and reluctant to recognise any limitation to gender equality based on religion, culture or custom.[60] CEDAW does not recognise a right to religious freedom and it actually requires states to modify cultural attitudes and beliefs to ensure gender equality.[61] The CEDAW Committee holds that 'no one may invoke cultural diversity to infringe upon human rights guaranteed by international law'.[62] Sex education is a powerful tool to dismantle negative cultural attitudes and norms on the roles of men and woman and is a transformative remedy to gender-based violence. These are fundamental human rights and the state has a legitimate aim in fulfilling these rights.

Prima facie, it would appear that CEDAW holds that conservative religious and cultural values cannot be used to limit the delivery of sex education which fulfils fundamental human rights for girls and women. A challenge however remains. The UN Special Rapporteur on the freedom of religion and belief notes that 'there is no general recipe for handling' the conflict between sex education and conservative religious or cultural-based oppositions.[63] Recognising that the freedom of belief and religion can be limited to ensure the gender equality does not provide any guidance on the exact parameters of this limitation.

Guidance can be found from regional courts which have been assessing claims for faith-based exemptions in the context of education. This jurisprudence provides helpful examples on how religion, custom, culture and gender equality can be balanced. The European Court of Human Rights (ECtHR) in *Dojan v Germany* did not allow faith-based exemptions to sex education in public school.[64] The Court relied on two contradictory characterisations of the state's aims to justify limiting the freedom of religion. First, the Court repeatedly describes the delivery of sex education as the neutral transmission of knowledge. This

---

[60] For a criticism of this position see Celestine Nyamu Musembi, 'Pulling apart? Treatment of pluralism and Maputo Protocol', in Anne Hellum and Henriette Sinding Aasen (eds) *Women's human rights: CEDAW in international, regional and national human rights*, Cambridge: Cambridge University Press, 2013.

[61] CEDAW, Article 5. See also Frances Raday, 'Traditionalist religious and cultural challengers – international and constitutional human rights responses', *Israel Law Review*, 14 (2008): 408.

[62] CEDAW Committee, General Recommendation No. 31: On harmful practices.

[63] UN Special Rapporteur on freedom of religion or belief, Report to the Human Rights Council (School education), UN Doc. A/HRC/16/53, 2011, para. 55.

[64] Application No. 319/08 (Admissibility).

is problematic as this justification for limiting the freedom of religion is based on neutrality. This has the potential to reduce sex education to biological facts and ignores the transformative aims. Second, the state argued that, by providing sex education, it was fulfilling its obligations under the right to education.[65] The Court carefully analysed the normative aims of the right to education – tolerance, diversity and critical thinking skills – and concluded that sex education furthered these goals. Any exemption to sex education would undermine the right. This is the stronger, more compelling argument. It is the weight of the human rights at stake, such as the right to education or gender equality, that explains why sex education is a positive obligation on the state and justifies the limitation on the freedom of religion and belief. This argument is more consistent with the understanding developed in the second section of this article, 'CEDAW's commitment to sex education', that to realise gender equality the state must provide sex education.

The ECtHR also held that the right to freedom of religion and belief was minimally restricted and that respect was still being shown to religious differences. The Court drew a distinction between public and private space. The parents 'were free to educate their children after school ... thus their right to educate their children in conformity with their religious convictions ...'[66] and the curriculum was not critical of different religious beliefs.[67] The Court noted that the right to freedom of belief or religion 'does not guarantee the right not to be confronted with opinions that are opposed to one's convictions'.[68] The ECtHR is engaging in a true assessment. It is not simply that sex education 'wins' and the right to freedom of religion 'loses'. There is still scope for religion and cultural beliefs but due to the fundamental human rights at stake, it cannot be used to justify limits on sex education in school.

How should the CEDAW Committee approach conservative religious and cultural norms in the context of sex education? The UN Special Rapporteur on religion recommends a soft approach that de-escalates conflict and reaches out towards particular communities.[69] A firm but conciliatory approach is crucial. First, the treaty bodies can recommend

[65] Protocol 1 to the European Convention on Human Rights, ETS 9 (entered into force 18 May 1954), Article 2.

[66] *Dojan* (n 64) 16.

[67] ibid. 7.

[68] ibid.15.

[69] UN Special Rapporteur on freedom of religion or belief, Report to the Human Rights Council (Equality between men and women), UN Doc. A/68/290, 2011, para. 55.

that the state build strategic relationships through dialogue with parents, community and religious leaders on the design and implementation of human rights-based sex education.[70] Consultation and the participation of diverse groups can ensure that unique and culturally sensitive solutions that have the support of powerful local actors, are developed to address conservative religious and cultural obstacles to sex education. Second, the state can address the concerns of conservative religious and cultural leaders and any misconceptualisations of sex education. For instance, there is often concern that sex education will increase the rates of sexual activity among young people and the state can demonstrate with evidence-based arguments that this is not the case.[71] Third, it can also be particularly helpful for the state to familiarise parents and community and religious leaders using evidence that sex education aims not to undermine religious and cultural norms but to protect and fulfil rights to gender equality and freedom from gender-based violence.[72] The main goal of a conciliatory approach is to establish and maintain respectful lines of communication between the relevant parties while at the same time ensuring the delivery of human rights-based sex education. However, the CEDAW Committee still must affirm the positive obligation on the state to provide sex education, regardless of conservative religious and cultural beliefs. It can express concern when it is evident that conservative religious and cultural norms are limiting sex education. And it can remind the state that the freedom of religion and belief needs to be limited so that the human rights of girls and women are fulfilled.

Establishing legal accountability mechanisms

The final obstacle that the treaty bodies need to address when evaluating the state's sex education programmes is the establishment of legal accountability mechanisms. Too frequently sex education is treated as an option. Recognising that sex education is linked to the fulfilment of gender equality means that the state needs to establish

---

[70] Report of the UN Special Rapporteur on the right to education, UN Doc. A/65/162, para. 87(h).

[71] Report of the UN Special Rapporteur on the right to education, UN Doc. A/65/162, para. 87(h).

[72] Report of the UN Special Rapporteur on the right to education, UN Doc. A/65/162, para. 87(h); Nicole Haberland, 'The case for addressing gender and power in sexuality and HIV education', *International Perspectives on Sexual and Reproductive Health*, 41(1) (2015): 311.

and maintain a transparent and effective monitoring system.[73] This is challenging when there are multiple educational structures that exist within the state: ranging from state to privately funded schools and the proliferation of public–private partnerships in education.[74] These new educational models tend to conceptualise education as a market good. They are often un- or poorly regulated and 'a human rights perspective is largely absent from the public discourse'.[75] However, the UN Special Rapporteur on the right to education reminds us that 'any arrangement … between the public (government) and the private (a private entrepreneur, enterprise or entity) is and remains subject to human rights laws'.[76] The state retains its human rights obligations and accountability 'even when outsourcing education to private actors'.[77]

The CEDAW Committee does not need to design or recommend a specific accountability system. The state has the choice between legislation, regulation, internal audits and other curriculum monitoring devices. The CEDAW Committee should remind the state that because sex education fulfils fundamental human rights, it must be properly monitored. In the context of the delivery of comprehensive sex education this also means that states cannot argue that they do not have an obligation to monitor private institutions. The treaty bodies can draw on the UN Special Rapporteur on the right to education's insights that the state cannot outsource its human rights obligations.

Conclusion

The lack of good-quality sex education can have a devastating effect on the lives of girls and women and perpetuate cycles of gender disadvantage. CEDAW offers new ways of conceptualising and addressing these challenges. There are specific obligations referring to sex education in the treaty and most importantly there is a positive obligation on the state to provide sex education to fulfil the fundamental

---

[73] See CESCR, General Comment No. 13: The right to education, E/C.12/1999/10, 1999, para. 49.

[74] UN Special Rapporteur on the right to education, Report to the UN General Assembly (Public–private partnerships), UN Doc. A/70/342, 2015.

[75] Helen Taylor, Laura Hilly and Meghan Campbell, 'Background paper to public–private partnerships', http://ohrh.law.ox.ac.uk/wordpress/wp-content/uploads/2015/07/Background-Paper1.pdf

[76] UN Special Rapporteur on the right to education, Report to the UN General Assembly (Public–private partnerships), para. 82.

[77] UN Special Rapporteur on the right to education, Report to the UN General Assembly (Public–private partnerships), para. 94.

rights of girls and women. Sex education is a necessary measure to ensure girls and women's right to life, health, education, gender equality and freedom from violence. A human rights perspective also brings clarity in how to address the obstacles to sex education. The CEDAW Committee, in its monitoring role, can recommend that the state approach sex education as an issue of human rights. This gives the CEDAW Committee the required tools to address the obstacles to sex education. It can draw on human rights norms to remind the state that there needs to be legal accountability, monitoring and mechanisms in place so that individuals can enforce the state's positive obligation to provide sex education regardless of the type of school they attend. Perhaps most importantly, a human rights approach offers a framework in which to mediate the role of conservative religious and cultural norms and the delivery of human rights-based sex education. Due to the significance of the human rights that are fulfilled by sex education, it is necessary and proportionate to limit the role of conservative religious and cultural norms in delivery of sex education in the classroom. Using the international human rights framework to reconceptualise sex education as a positive obligation necessary to fulfil human rights can help ensure that women and girls are able to live empowered and equal lives.

Part IV
Litigating for quality and equality in education

Conceptualising and enforcing the right to quality education for minorities and disadvantaged groups: reflections on the Campaign for Fiscal Equity litigation

Helen Taylor

Introduction: achieving access to quality education for all

Over the last fifteen years, there has been a gradual shift in focus from *access* to *quality* within the international drive for realising the human right to education. The dominant focus on access to education at the turn of the century was reflected in the target of universal primary education established by Millennium Development Goal 2 and initiatives like Education for All,[1] the UNICEF-led movement that coordinates and supports international efforts to universalise primary education. Much progress has been made on this front, with enrolment in primary education in developing regions reaching 91% in 2015, a considerable improvement from 83% in 2000.[2] However, although access is a necessary condition for realising the right to education, it is on its own not sufficient. Rather, access must be accompanied by the opportunity to obtain quality education, if education is to be a 'multiplier' or 'enabling' right that empowers people to live productive and fulfilling lives in society. This realisation has shaped the more nuanced target of Sustainable Development Goal 4 to ensure inclusive and quality education for all. This more refined aim of quality education

---

[1]   The movement was launched at the World Conference on Education for All in 1990, where participants pledged themselves to universalising primary education, and six key education goals for achieving this global commitment by 2015 were laid out at the World Education Forum in 2000.

[2]   See www.un.org/millenniumgoals/education.shtml.

for all is particularly important for ensuring *equality* in education, as an assessment of the discrepancies in the quality of education provided is often more telling of inequality in education, and in society more generally, than the all-or-nothing measure of access. The shift in focus towards quality of education is therefore highly relevant to the enforcement of the right to education for minorities and disadvantaged groups. Yet while this shift in emphasis presents a valuable opportunity for ensuring greater equality in education provision, it brings with it the challenge of how to conceptualise and enforce the right to quality education for minorities and disadvantaged groups.

This chapter will explore how this focus on ensuring quality education for all can strengthen both the conceptualisation and enforcement of the right to education for minorities and disadvantaged groups. In drawing this link between quality and equality in education, I will address two questions. First, I will consider what a human rights-based assessment of quality brings to our conception of the right to education, with a particular interest in the strategic value it may hold for minorities and disadvantaged groups in realising their right to education. This question therefore concerns the role of quality within our conceptualisation of the normative content of the right to education. The second question draws out the implications of this conceptualisation of quality education for determining what the court's role should be in enforcing the right to education. This enquiry will consider how the court can design remedies that include accountability mechanisms to monitor the quality of education being provided as a result of the remedial relief granted.

I will bring these questions into sharper focus by exploring them within a concrete case, using the Campaign for Fiscal Equity litigation in the New York State courts as a case study.[3] The Campaign for Fiscal Equity litigation, which dealt with the constitutionality of New York State's education financing scheme, clearly demonstrates the strategic value that a human rights-based assessment of quality holds

---

[3]   My discussion will be limited to the three decisions by the New York Court of Appeals in 1995, 2003 and 2006, which for ease of reference I will call *CFE I*, *CFE II* and *CFE III* respectively: *Campaign for Fiscal Equity, Inc. v State*, 86 NY 2d 307 (NY 1995) (*CFE I*), *Campaign for Fiscal Equity, Inc. v State*, 100 NY 2d 893 (NY 2003) (*CFE II*) and *Campaign for Fiscal Equity, Inc. v State*, 861 NE 2d 51 (NY 2006) (*CFE III*). For clarity's sake, it is worth specifying the hierarchy of courts in New York State as they relate to this extended public interest litigation. At each of the three stages of the Campaign for Fiscal Equity litigation, the case was first heard by the Supreme Court (which I refer to as the trial court), then the Appellate Division, before finally reaching the Court of Appeals (which is the focus of my analysis).

for ensuring equality in education provision. While the plaintiffs' argument based on education equality failed, their successful claim based on education adequacy indirectly helped to ensure a more equitable allocation of funding to public schools in New York City. The litigation also demonstrates the close link and challenges between the conceptualisation of the right to quality education and the court's role when enforcing it. The causal relationship between New York State's education financing system and the adequacy of educational opportunities it provides, meant the courts had to engage with the polycentric question of education financing when granting remedial relief while being careful not to exceed the bounds of their legitimacy and expertise.

Conceptualising the right to quality education: the value of a human rights-based assessment of quality

The Campaign for Fiscal Equity litigation: a tale of two claims

The plaintiffs in the Campaign for Fiscal Equity litigation comprised a cross-section of stakeholders. The action was spearheaded by the Campaign for Fiscal Equity, Inc., a not-for-profit corporation whose membership consists of community school boards, individual citizens, and a number of parent advocacy organisations. They were joined by 14 of New York City's 32 school districts as well as individual students who attended New York City public schools and their parents. The context for their complaint was the underfunding of inner city schools which gave rise to noticeable discrepancies in educational opportunities and quality between schools with mostly disadvantaged and ethnic minority students, and those schools in more privileged districts that drew from a wealthier, largely white student base. Having met with no success in advocating for budgetary reforms through the political process, the plaintiffs resorted to litigation to challenge the constitutionality of the state's education financing scheme.

The plaintiffs put forward two main claims: one based on education equality and the other based on education adequacy. First, they challenged the state's formula for allocating funds to public schools. They argued that it had a disparate impact on racial and ethnic minorities and thus violated the Department of Education's implementing regulations for Title VI of the Civil Rights Act of 1964,[4] which prohibit policies that disproportionately harm a racial minority and that cannot be

---

[4]   42 USC §2000d (1964).

educationally justified by a legitimate non-discriminatory reason. This education *equality* claim was accompanied by a challenge based on the adequacy of the education being provided, in terms of which the plaintiffs alleged that the state's education financing scheme breached the right to education entrenched in the New York State Constitution. Article XI §1 (the Education Article) of the State Constitution requires that '[t]he legislature shall provide for the maintenance and support of a system of free common schools, wherein all the children of this state may be educated', but the plaintiffs alleged that the state was failing to provide New York City public school students with the opportunity to obtain a sound basic education. This claim therefore concerned the *quality* of education being received by students in the city's public schools.

The failure of the equality claim: a strategic loss and an expressive harm

The litigation played out in three main stages over a period of 13 years, with each sequence of appeals eventually reaching the New York Court of Appeals. The plaintiffs' Title VI claim based on education equality failed when the Court of Appeals held in *CFE II* that there is no private right of action under Title VI and thus did not address the merits of the discrimination claim.[5] The equality claim therefore failed at the outset, in spite of the clear evidence that the state's school funding formula resulted in an inequitable distribution of educational resources that had a disproportionately harmful effect on minority students relative to their white counterparts.

Denise Morgan, who represented the Black, Puerto Rican and Hispanic Legislative Caucus in the litigation, has made a strong argument for why the failure of the plaintiffs' Title VI claim is both strategically and theoretically significant.[6] Most obviously, the rejection of the Title VI claim signals the demise of one of the more promising federal litigation strategies for ensuring access to quality education for all children in the United States, but especially for minorities and disadvantaged groups. As Morgan highlights, Title VI claims have been

---

[5]   The Court of Appeals confirmed the reasoning behind the rejection of the Title VI claim as set out by the Appellate Division in *Campaign for Fiscal Equity, Inc. v State*, 801 NE2d 326 (2002), which relied on the precedent laid down by the US Supreme Court in *Alexander v Sandoval*, 532 US 275 (2001).

[6]   Denise Morgan, 'Campaign for Fiscal Equity, Inc. v. New York: no slam dunk victory for public school children', *Fordham Urban Law Journal*, 31 (2003): 1291–301.

relied on to challenge a myriad of educational issues affecting children of colour, including the placement of Black children in remedial classes, the failure of school districts to provide appropriate programmes for children whose first language is not English, and, of course, the disparate impact of public school funding schemes.[7] The more serious consequence of the courts' rejection of the Title VI claim, however, is the particular harm of not recognising the race-based injury which the plaintiffs proved at trial. As Morgan points out, only the plaintiffs' federal claim 'takes into account the particular injuries caused by the unjustified misdistribution of government resources by race, the harm to communities of colour, and the harm to our democratic society'.[8]

The success of the adequacy claim: defining a constitutional standard of quality

While this failure of the education equality claim was indeed a setback to the goal of ensuring quality education for all, the success of the plaintiff's education adequacy claim has resulted in significant progress towards a more equitable distribution of state funds for public schools in New York City. The education adequacy claim succeeded because the Court of Appeals in *CFE II* found that the state had failed to fulfil its positive duty to provide all students with a sound basic education as required by the Education Article of the New York State Constitution. Holding that there is a constitutional floor with regard to education adequacy, the Court of Appeals relied on the meaning of a 'sound basic education' that they had fleshed out in *CFE I*, namely 'the basic literacy, calculating, and verbal skills necessary to enable children to eventually function productively as civic participants capable of voting and serving on a jury'.[9] While education can be delivered according to a variety of models, these basic standards of quality must always be met. By insisting that these basic standards of quality be met in all schools, the Court of Appeals in *CFE II* indirectly addressed the problem of inequitable distribution of state funds, since the state's failure to provide a 'sound basic education' in all New York City public schools was attributed to their insufficient funding. The right to quality education was therefore an indirect way of tackling the inequality of educational provision between the more privileged, predominantly white schools and the relatively disadvantaged, predominantly non-white schools.

[7] Morgan, 'Campaign for Fiscal Equity, Inc.', 1300.
[8] Morgan, 'Campaign for Fiscal Equity, Inc.', 1301.
[9] *CFE I* at 316.

A particularly important feature of the Court of Appeal's finding in *CFE II* was that the distributive question of school funding was considered a key determinant of the quality of educational opportunity the school is able to offer. This causal relationship between the state's education financing system and the adequacy of educational opportunities it provides, meant the Court of Appeals had to engage with the polycentric question of education financing in order to define and adjudicate the right to education. Because funding is linked to quality, as an aspect of the normative content of the right to education, the state has a positive obligation to provide the constitutionally required funding for a sound basic education. The significance of this finding, as Fredman reflects, is that budgetary allocations are to be based on human rights, rather than human rights being made conditional upon budgets.[10] This clearly demonstrates the value of a human rights-based assessment of quality, since it ensures education funding is a positive human rights duty rather than simply a distributive decision left to the complete discretion of policy makers. The government cannot rely on budgetary constraints to justify their failure to provide education that meets the constitutional standard of quality, as education funding is not a purely political decision immune from judicial scrutiny, but rather a constitutional duty for which the courts have a responsibility to hold them to account.

Enforcing the right to quality education: implications for the role of the court

Designing remedies for enforcing the right to quality education: CFE II

This conceptualisation of the right to education, which includes a constitutional standard of quality, holds significant implications for the court's role in enforcing the right to education. By articulating basic standards of quality as being a constitutional minimum, the Court of Appeals was also recognising the state's positive duty to supply the constitutionally required funding for providing education of that quality. In this way, the court was drawn into enforcing the state's obligations in respect of education financing, but had to be careful that its engagement with this polycentric question did not exceed the bounds of its legitimacy and expertise. Having found that the

---

[10] Sandra Fredman, *Human rights transformed: Positive rights and positive duties*, Oxford: Oxford University Press, 2008, p 219.

state's existing education financing scheme fell short of providing the quality of education required by the New York State Constitution, the Court of Appeals in *CFE II* then had the difficult task of deciding what remedial relief to order. There was heated disagreement among the justices of the Court of Appeals on this issue, as they were torn between their judicial responsibility to provide effective remedial relief, on the one hand, and the proper limits of the judicial role in having 'neither the authority, nor the ability, nor the will, to micromanage education financing',[11] on the other.

Chief Judge Kaye, delivering the Opinion of the Court in *CFE II*, recognised the importance of deference in matters of fiscal policy but nevertheless maintained that there were remedial possibilities capable of providing effective relief which did not require courts to step outside their proper role. The remedial order she granted required the state to ascertain the actual cost of providing a 'sound basic education' in New York City, and to reform the current education financing system so that every school would have sufficient resources to provide the opportunity for children to acquire a 'sound basic education'.[12] Importantly, her remedial order did not impose the court's view of what amount was required for the state to fulfil its obligations in respect of education financing, but instead set the constitutional standard for what would constitute a 'sound basic education' and required the government to put in place a budget that would achieve that standard. The remedy thus did not require the court to 'micromanage education financing'[13] but it did lay down a clear constitutional standard of quality together with guidance for how it should be implemented.

A crucial aspect of the remedial order was the requirement that the reforms include an accountability mechanism for evaluating whether the reforms were in fact achieving the goal of providing a 'sound basic education'.[14] Chief Judge Kaye recognised that an effective remedy would need to monitor the quality of education being delivered as a result of the reforms, and she therefore granted the trial court supervisory jurisdiction to provide a measure of guidance and accountability to the government's implementation of the remedial order. By designing the remedy in this way, Chief Judge Kaye clearly anticipated meaningful dialogue and cooperation between the courts and the legislature in the enforcement of the right to quality education – she firmly placed

[11]   *CFE II* at 925.
[12]   *CFE II* at 930.
[13]   *CFE II* at 925.
[14]   *CFE II* at 930.

the responsibility for reforming the education financing scheme with the state legislature, but maintained a supervisory role for the trial court to ensure the reforms comply with the constitutional standard of quality it has set out.

Responding to non-compliance: CFE III

While *CFE II* addressed the question of the appropriate role of the court in the remedial process, the Court of Appeals in *CFE III* was confronted with the question of the appropriate judicial response to non-compliance. Although the government had made some changes to education financing,[15] they had failed to implement all the required budgetary reforms within the deadline set by Chief Judge Kaye in *CFE II*. In the face of this substantial non-compliance, the trial court resorted to appointing an independent panel of referees to evaluate government compliance and propose a budgetary model that would ensure public schools are sufficiently funded to provide an adequate education to its students. On appeal, however, the majority of the Court of Appeals held in *CFE III* that the trial court had intruded on the government's domain by appointing a panel of referees. In many ways, this was a disappointing end to the long battle by the Campaign for Fiscal Equity, as the Court of Appeals allowed the normative commitment embodied in the right to education to be undermined by the government's non-compliance with its remedial order. Without effective remedial relief, the groundbreaking judicial opinion by Chief Judge Kaye in *CFE II* remains a hollow victory, without concrete and tangible effect beyond the courtroom. This is particularly true in public interest litigation involving minorities and disadvantaged groups for whom access to justice is often hard to obtain, such as the children in New York City's public schools. For them, the 'cash value' of the right to education amounts to the effective remedial relief they obtain,[16] such that *CFE III* leaves them with very little indeed.

There is, however, a less obvious but equally important insight into the court's role in enforcing the right to quality education. Although the government failed to comply with most of the directives of the remedial order handed down in *CFE II*, some significant steps had

---

[15]   There had been some reform of the system, in that the legislature had passed a budget increasing capital expenditure, but the rest of the education financing system remained unchanged.

[16]   Daryl Levinson, 'Rights essentialism and remedial equilibration', *Columbia Law Review*, 99 (1999): 857–940 at 874.

been taken to improve the education financing scheme as a result of the earlier litigation in *CFE I* and *CFE II*. In particular, legislation had been passed to increase the budget for capital expenditure such that the Court of Appeals in *CFE III* considered it unnecessary to make any further order in this regard.[17] With hindsight, therefore, it is clear that the Court's adjudication of the state's positive duty to make available sufficient financial resources to cover the costs of providing a 'sound basic education' grounded a political process that sought to improve the education financing system. Seen in this light, the Court's approach can be viewed as a persuasive model for how its remedial response can prompt the government to act on the obligations identified by the Court.

This insight highlights the fact that the Court never acts in isolation of political actors in strategic public interest litigation. On the contrary, Gauri and Brinks point out that 'courts themselves are deeply implicated in [a] set of strategic interactions'[18] and that it is 'precisely because they are never fully independent of political pressures' that they can 'help overcome political blockages, channel important information to political and bureaucratic actors, create spaces of deliberation and compromise between competing interests, and hold states accountable to incomplete commitments'.[19] Arguably, the Court of Appeals in *CFE III* should have been bolder in its responsibility to ensure its remedial orders are enforced, but the longer perspective demonstrates that the Campaign for Fiscal Equity litigation did nevertheless prompt significant progress in providing access to quality education for all children in New York City's public schools.

Conclusion

The Campaign for Fiscal Equity litigation demonstrates the value of a human rights-based assessment of quality for ensuring quality education for all. While direct reliance on discrimination failed, the plaintiffs' challenge to the adequacy of education in New York City's public schools indirectly exposed the discrepancy in the quality of education being received by disadvantaged and ethnic minority students as opposed to wealthier, mostly white students. Without overlooking

---

[17] *CFE III* at 57.
[18] V. Gauri and D.M. Brinks (eds), *Courting social justice: Judicial enforcement of social and economic rights in the developing world*, Cambridge: Cambridge University Press, 2008, p 4.
[19] Gauri and Brinks, *Courting social justice*, p 6.

the expressive harm suffered by minority and disadvantaged students as a result of the Court not recognising their race-based injury, the conceptualisation of the right to education as including a constitutional standard of quality was strategically valuable in achieving a more equitable distribution of education financing. This success of the Campaign for Fiscal Equity litigation serves as a valuable lesson in the potential use of a quality claim for challenging inequality in education. This is particularly relevant in jurisdictions, like the United States, where equality is conceptualised in formal, rather than substantive, terms. However, a human rights-based assessment of quality can only ensure greater equality in education where quality is conceptualised in meaningful terms, otherwise there is a risk that a very thin conception of quality could in fact lead to a 'levelling down' rather than 'levelling up' of standards. An appreciation of education as a 'multiplier' or 'enabling' right, that is, one that empowers people to live productive and fulfilling lives in society, is a promising point of departure for any human rights-based assessment of quality.

Beyond this strategic benefit, however, the value of a human rights-based assessment of quality lies in its implications for the obligations of the government in realising the right to education. By assessing quality according to constitutional standards, the provision of quality education for all is recognised as a positive duty that the state is constitutionally obliged to fulfil, rather than simply a distributive decision left to the unfettered discretion of policy makers. Since education financing is surely one of the most important, but also one of the most controversial, aspects of ensuring the provision of quality education, the justiciability of the state's obligations in this regard is a powerful tool for realising the right to education through public interest litigation on behalf of minorities and disadvantaged groups. In jurisdictions where the state neglects its positive obligations towards minorities and disadvantaged groups, a human rights-based conceptualisation of quality can strengthen the enforcement of the right to education by crystallising the state's constitutional obligations.

Finally, a human rights-based assessment of quality also holds important implications for the role of the courts when enforcing the right to quality education. The state's failure to provide education of adequate quality requires the court to provide effective remedial relief for rights holders, in keeping with its responsibility to ensure the right to education is enforced. Although courts enjoy judicial independence, their decisions always take place within a matrix of strategic interactions, with the result that they will be most effective when they are sensitive and responsive to the broader sociopolitical context within which the education litigation is brought. While this is admittedly a challenging task for the courts, it is one that they are uniquely placed to fulfil.

NINE

From the classroom to the courtroom: litigating education rights in South Africa

Jason Brickhill and Yana van Leeve[1]

Introduction

In his swansong judgment for the South African Constitutional Court, the erstwhile Deputy Chief Justice Dikgang Moseneke articulated the link between systems of oppression and access to education:

> All forms of human oppression and exclusion are premised, in varying degrees, on a denial of access to education and training. The uneven power relations that marked slavery, colonialism, the industrial age and the information economy are girded, in great part, by inadequate access to quality teaching and learning.[2]

Education is thus important for human dignity, equality, livelihood and democracy. Indeed, the transformative and aspirational nature of the Constitution gives a unique role to courts in South Africa to be crucial contributors on matters of public policy, traditionally within the exclusive terrain of the executive branch of government. Since its establishment in 1993, the Constitutional Court has made bold rulings to uphold fundamental rights; abolishing the death penalty,[3]

---

[1] We are grateful for helpful comments on earlier drafts of this piece from Sanya Samtani and Nurina Ally, as well as the valuable input of the editors of this collection. The responsibility for any remaining errors is ours.

[2] *Federation of Governing Bodies for South African Schools (FEDSAS) v Member of the Executive Council for Education, Gauteng and Another* 2016 (4) SA 546 (CC) at para. 3.

[3] *S v Makwanyane* 1995 (3) SA 391 (CC).

recognising same-sex marriage[4] and compelling the state to permit and facilitate the use of the antiretroviral drug, nevirapine in order to reduce the risk of mother-to-child transmission of HIV.[5] More recently, the Constitutional Court has also extended a commercial contract between the state and a private entity to which government had outsourced the function of paying social assistance, in order to ensure the continued payment of grants to the most vulnerable people in South Africa's deeply unequal society.[6] Most of these progressive gains have been achieved through proactive, strategically minded litigants seeking to give effect to recognised rights in the Constitution and overturn discriminatory laws and practices.

The Constitution confers substantial power upon courts to enforce justiciable socioeconomic rights, including the rights to housing, health care, food and social security, which are to be guaranteed to all people and which require the state to take positive measures to realise the right for those who bear the brunt of structural poverty and inequality. The right to education, guaranteed in section 29 of the Constitution, is in several respects an even more robust right than the other socioeconomic rights in the Constitution.

Section 29 of the Constitution confers an unqualified right on every person to a 'basic education, including adult basic education'.[7] Similarly, every individual has the right to 'further education'. However, the state only has to take reasonable measures to 'progressively realise' the right to further education. To promote the accessibility and appropriateness of education, everyone has the right to receive education at a public institution in an official language or language of their choice, where practicable. Furthermore, this must be guaranteed by the state having regard to principles of equity and the constitutional imperative to redress the imbalances and injustices caused by racially discriminatory

---

4   *Minister of Home Affairs v Fourie* 2006 (1) SA524 (CC). This was preceded by *National Coalition for Gay and Lesbian Equality and Another v Minister of Justice and Others* 1999 (1) SA 6 invalidating laws criminalising sex between men.

5   *Minister of Health and Others v Treatment Action Campaign and Others* (No. 2) 2002 (5) SA 721.

6   *AllPay Consolidated Investment Holdings (Pty) Ltd v Chief Executive Officer, South African Social Security Agency* 2014 (1) SA 604 (CC) (setting aside a state contract to provide services for the payment of social grants) and *Black Sash Trust v Minister of Social Development and Others* 2017 (3) SA 335 (CC) (declaring that the private party was under a constitutional obligation to provide social assistance, notwithstanding the invalidity of the state contract).

7   Section 29 of the Constitution provides as follows: 'Everyone has the right: (a) To basic education, including adult basic education; (b) To further education which the State through reasonable measures must make progressively available and accessible.'

laws and practices. Sections 29(3) and (4) of the Constitution permit the establishment of private (independent) educational institutions that may claim an entitlement to state subsidies in certain circumstances.[8] Recognising these constituent elements, the right is comprehensively formulated and understood by the courts as an 'empowerment right' that is necessary for each individual to develop their abilities and access social and economic opportunities.[9]

The realisation of the right to a 'basic education' has dominated education rights litigation, with little focus so far on adult, tertiary and vocational training. The focus on basic education is likely due to the impact it has on all children, and the Constitution's special protection of children's interests.[10] A further explanation could include the vast disparities in education provision and the fatal consequences of inadequate basic school infrastructure.[11]

In ordinary parlance, 'basic education' in South Africa refers to education in a person's primary and secondary schooling years, from grade R, the year in which a student starts formal schooling, until grade 12, the year in which the South African school leaving 'matriculation'

---

[8] *KwaZulu-Natal Joint Liaison Committee v MEC Department of Education, Kwazulu-Natal and Others* 2013 (4) SA 262 (CC); Norms and Standards for School Funding Government Gazette 29179, Government Notice 869, 31 August 2006, promulgated in terms of the South African Schools Act No. 84 of 1996 includes norms for both public and independent schools.

[9] *Governing Body of the Juma Musjid Primary School & Others v Essay N.O. and Others* 2011 (8) BCLR 761 (CC) at paras. 41–3. *Madzodzo and Others v Minister of Basic Education and Others* 2014 (3) SA 441 (ECM) at para. 18.

[10] Section 28(2) of the Constitution provides that: 'A child's best interests are of paramount importance in every matter concerning the child.' In 2015 there were approximately 14.1 million students at school. There is almost universal school attendance in the age group 7–15 years, however after that attendance drops rapidly. See General Household Survey 2015 conducted by Statistics South Africa: www.statssa.gov.za/publications/P0318/P03182015.pdf.

[11] In 2014, 6-year-old Michael Komape drowned in a pit toilet while at school in Limpopo Province, one of South Africa's poorest and most under-resourced areas. See M. Heywood, 'Our national shame: in memory of Michael Komape, 2009–2014', *Daily Maverick*, 23 January 2015, www.dailymaverick.co.za/opinionista/2015-01-23-our-national-shame-in-memory-of-michael-komape-2009-2014/#.WQLq5vl96M8.

examinations are taken,[12] or, more conservatively, the compulsory school going ages between 7 and 14.

For most children, the education system is endured in tough physical conditions, characterised by unsafe facilities owing to massive infrastructure backlogs, insufficient teaching and learning materials, unreliable transport and serious deficits in teacher content knowledge.[13] More fundamentally, the likelihood of teachers being absent from the classroom is a serious concern, as are concerns of safety from crime, gang violence and sexual violence in schools.[14] These experiences are magnified in the urban townships and rural areas that have been historically underserviced and under-resourced. The causes of these conditions are vast and beyond the scope of this chapter. However, it is clear that the roots lie in the country's colonial and apartheid history. Today, the crisis is exacerbated by the continuing weakening of public education and the increasing commodification and privatisation of education by both for-profit and non-profit interests. We do not discount private provision of education, nor do we ignore the plethora of ways in which the private sector is presently involved in public education. However, the perception that low-fee private institutions

[12] Children in South Africa are obliged to attend school from the age of 7, ordinarily grade 1, and may leave school from the age of 15 or grade 9, whichever occurs first. Section 3(3) South African Schools Act No. 84 of 1996 places a statutory obligation on the public authority to ensure that every child of compulsory school age is placed in a school. Consequently, sanctions follow if anyone prevents a child of compulsory school age from attending school.

[13] H. Venkat and N. Spaull, 'What do we know about primary teachers' mathematical content knowledge in South Africa? An analysis of SACMEQ 2007', *International Journal of Education Development*, 41(C) (2015): 121–30; N. Spaull, 'Accountability in South African education', in Jan Hofmeyr and Ayanda Nyoka (eds) *Transformation audit 2013: Confronting exclusion*, 2013, www.ijr.org.za/portfolio-items/transformation-audit-2013-confronting-exclusion/.

[14] Notwithstanding these challenges, South Africa's democratic government has adopted a legislative framework that gives content to the education right. It has adopted progressive policies, including the National School Nutrition Programme which provides over 9 million students with state-subsidised nutritious meals at school every day, as well as expanding the grade R programmes resulting in greatly improved enrolment for pre-primary school students; adopting binding minimum uniform norms and standards for school infrastructure that prescribe the basic infrastructure norms for all schools; and expanding the number of no-fee schools, enabling students in the poorest schools to attend schools for free. For an overview of the status of the right to education in South Africa, see S. Franklin and D. McLaren, *Realising the right to basic education in South Africa: An analysis of the content, policy effort, resource allocation and enjoyment of the constitutional right to a basic education*, www.spii.org.za/wp-content/uploads/2015/11/2015-SPII-Realising-the-Right-to-a-Basic-Education-in-SouthAfrica.pdf.

are able to provide a solution to challenges in the public education system is overstated.[15] This is illustrated in the two biggest costs in education – teacher remuneration (personnel expenditure) and infrastructure – which low-fee private schools are unable to maintain in the same way as the state or, more importantly, with the same system of accountability and social protections to ensure maximum protection of students' and workers' rights.[16] The consequence is that these low-fee private schools make compromises in critical areas while, at the same time, claiming an entitlement to public resources, instead of trying to contribute towards building a quality education for all.[17] Although Smuts' chapter in this collection makes a case for the positive value of non-profit private providers, we note that many of the issues that arise in the context of for-profit private providers are equally applicable to non-profit providers.[18]

This chapter focuses on two streams of education litigation concerning public schools in South Africa: first, cases concerning contestation over the power to formulate policy for schools in the education system established in the new democratic era; and, second, cases seeking to compel the state to provide specific education inputs

---

[15] I. Macphearson, S. Robertson and G. Waldorf (eds) *Education, privatisation and social justice: Case studies from Africa, South Asia and South East Asia*, Didcot: Symposium, 2014.

[16] Y. van Leeve, 'Executive heavy handedness and the right to basic education: a reply to Sandra Fredman', *Constitutional Court Review 6* (2014); Centre for Development Enterprise, *The financial viability of low-fee private schools in South Africa*, Johannesburg, 2015 at 11, www.cde.org.za/wp-content/uploads/2015/07/INVESTING-IN-POTENTIALFull-Report.pdf.

[17] In *KwaZulu-Natal Joint Liaison Committee v MEC Department of Education, Kwazulu-Natal and Others*, the Constitutional Court upheld a claim by an association of low-free private schools to receive a state subsidy after the due date for the payment of the promised subsidy had passed.

[18] J. Hofmeyr and I. McCay, 'Private education for the poor: more, different and better', *Journal of the Helen Suzman Foundation* 56 (2010) at 54, hsf.org.za/resource-centre/focus/focus-56-february-2010-on-learning-and-teaching/focus-56-february-2010.

(textbooks, furniture, teachers, infrastructure and scholar transport).[19] In the next section, we provide a brief overview of the structural inequalities in the education system left by apartheid legislation that key stakeholders in the current education dispensation have attempted to redress, and we explain in the following section how this has given rise to a stream of litigation centred on the power dynamics in controlling access to quality public schools. In the subsequent section, we explore a second stream of education litigation that has focused on physical education inputs. Through strategic litigation, the judicial process has stimulated new coalitions within civil society to mobilise around the education right, particularly among grassroots community organisations and public interest law centres.

Leaving the legacy behind

The Bantu Education Act of 1953 was one of several laws that shaped the Nationalist government's policy of apartheid between 1948 and 1990 to maintain white superiority and ensure the subservience of Black people, Africans in particular, through racial segregation in education.[20] Included among the forms of regulation were the Population Registration Act and the Group Areas Act of 1950, as well as the Natives Act of 1952. Together, this system of regulation classified people according to four main racial groups – white, African, Indian and 'coloured' – and conferred a power on the government to declare

---

[19] For a useful research report on education litigation in South Africa, see the Open Society Justice Initiative, *Strategic Litigation Impacts: Equal Access to Quality Education*, New York: Open Society Foundation, 2017. A third stream of litigation, which we have not discussed in this piece, concerns the experience of students at school and how the right to education is being constituted in relation to safety and security at school, gender and sexual orientation, and appropriate disciplinary practices. In an early piece at a stage when this body of litigation was only beginning to unfold, Skelton made a number of predictions about education rights litigation that proved largely accurate: that the courts would not be impeded in enforcing the education right by the doctrine of the separation of powers; that the courts would not adopt the 'reasonableness' approach to this right; that the courts might employ the limitations clause in Section 36 of the Constitution to temper the immediately realisable nature of the right; and that the courts would employ creative and participatory remedies in enforcing the right. See Ann Skelton, 'How far will the courts go in ensuring the right to a basic education?' *South African Public Law*, 27 (2012): 392–408.

[20] Linda Chisholm, 'Apartheid education legacies and new directions in post-apartheid South Africa', *Storia delle donne*, 8 (2012), www.storiadelledonne.it/wp-content/uploads/2009/03/chisholm2012.pdf.

148

geographical areas exclusive to particular racial groups.[21] In this way, the Nationalist government stunted the development of Black youth and controlled the movement of Black people and the types of work they could pursue.[22]

This undoubtedly had a massive negative impact upon the access to, and the quality of, education of African, Indian and coloured people in South Africa. Through the Bantu Education Act, African children in particular were the worst off, educated in separate school environments in dramatically inferior and rudimentary conditions, relative to white, coloured and Indian children. One need look no further than to observe the racial differentials in the level of qualifications offered and the quality of teacher training. As Chisholm notes, in '1965, only 25.5% of African teachers had university degrees'.[23] Spending on Black children, relative to white children was similarly disparate. In 1960 the Nationalist government spent eleven times as much on a white child as it did on a Black child.[24] The quality of school education for Black children, through insidious design, could never be equal to that of their white counterparts.

This segregated school system, in which public resources were concentrated on educating white children, has given way to a formally integrated, but in reality bifurcated system in the democratic era. Today, formerly white public schools provide quality schooling for the country's middle class of all races (but predominantly white and Indian children); while schools originally established for Black students in the rural areas and urban townships (characterised by informal and densely populated housing settlements in and around cities) continue to serve almost exclusively those communities and are massively

[21] Under the Population Registration Act, Coloured and Indian people were formally classified into various perpetual and absurd subgroups: Cape Coloured, Malay, Griqua, Chinese, Other Asian and Other Coloured.
[22] Black oppression did not start with apartheid, formally introduced in 1948. As far back as the early 1920s Black people were systematically excluded from the equal protection and benefit of the law. For example, the Minimum Wages Act of 1925 aimed to introduce minimum wage standards for whites only; the Transvaal Dealers (Control) Ordinance No. 11 of 1925 restricted the trade of Indian people and the Industrial Conciliation Act No. 11 of 1924 excluded Black people from membership of registered trade unions and prohibited registration of Black trade unions.
[23] Chisholm, 'Apartheid education legacies', at 86.
[24] Pam Christie and Colin Collins, 'Bantu education: apartheid ideology or labour reproduction?', *Comparative Education*, 18(1) (1982): 59–75.

under-resourced and frequently dysfunctional.[25] The ongoing de facto segregation in South Africa's schools can be attributed to the ongoing spectre of racial inequality reflected in the composition of socioeconomic classes.[26]

In the era following the adoption of the interim Constitution in 1994, the law changed radically, but the inequalities and fragmentation created by the apartheid education system remained. Although significant strides have been made, chronic resource and capacity constraints persist. These conditions have created fertile ground for the growth of a national movement of students, parents and teachers campaigning for equal education and increasing litigation to improve access to quality education.

Players and powers: who gets to set school policies?

South Africa's democratic government sought to open the doors of learning and culture to all by replacing a racially fragmented education system with a single national education department.[27] In *Hoërskool*

---

[25] Nic Spaull, 'Schooling in South Africa: how low-quality education becomes a poverty trap', in A. De Lannoy, S. Swartz, L. Lake and C. Smith (eds) *South African Child Gauge* 2015. Cape Town: Children's Institute, University of Cape Town, 2015.

[26] According to Franklin and McLaren, *Realising the right to basic education in South Africa*, at 146: 'The gap in Grade 12 attainment has dropped the most between Indian and White South Africans, where Indian adults went from being 23% less likely to complete Grade 12 than White adults in 2002 to being approximately 13% less likely in 2014. Gaps between White and Black South Africans in terms of completing Grade 12 have been much slower to close with differences in Grade 12 attainment improving only marginally between 2002 and 2014 from 48% to just below 43%.'

[27] The Freedom Charter was adopted at the Congress of the People at Kliptown, Johannesurg in 1955. It represented a clear and powerful statement of the vision for South Africa's future. The statement for equal education reads in relevant part: 'The Doors of Learning and Culture Shall be Opened!; The government shall discover, develop and encourage national talent for the enhancement of our cultural life; All the cultural treasures of mankind shall be open to all, by free exchange of books, ideas and contact with other lands; The aim of education shall be to teach the youth to love their people and their culture, to honour human brotherhood, liberty and peace; Education shall be free, compulsory, universal and equal for all children; Higher education and technical training shall be opened to all by means of state allowances and scholarships awarded on the basis of merit; Adult illiteracy shall be ended by a mass state education plan; Teachers shall have all the rights of other citizens; The colour bar in cultural life, in sport and in education shall be abolished.' See: www.historicalpapers.wits.ac.za/inventories/inv_pdfo/AD1137/AD1137-Ea6-1-001-jpeg.pdf.

Ermelo, the Constitutional Court identified the key stakeholders within the legal framework of South Africa's education system as the national and provincial government and school governing bodies:

> An overarching design of the Act is that public schools are run by three crucial partners. The national government is represented by the Minister for Education whose primary role is to set uniform norms and standards for public schools. The provincial government acts through the [Provincial Minister] for Education who bears the obligation to establish and provide public schools and, together with the Head of the Provincial Department of Education, exercises executive control over public schools through principals. Parents of the students and members of the community in which the school is located are represented in the school governing body which exercises defined autonomy over some of the domestic affairs of the school.[28]

The introduction of school governing bodies was a key feature in the creation of a model of governance that fosters consensus building and inclusion in the running of a school's affairs.

In this regard, such bodies exercise wide statutory powers, principally under the South African Schools Act 84 of 1996, to adopt policies that determine access to the schooling system. In flexing their financial power, they may determine compulsory uncapped fees and fee exemption criteria for certain families.[29] Although the South African Schools Act provides that children may not be removed from school on the basis that their fees are unpaid, school fees generally represent an economic barrier for admission to the school in the first instance. This leaves parents with little choice but to send their children to free, that is non-fee-paying, public schools that are usually overcrowded

---

[28] *Head of Department: Mpumalanga Department of Education and Another v Hoërskool Ermelo and Another* 2010 (2) SA 415 (CC) at para. 56 (henceforth *Hoërskool Ermelo*) (footnotes omitted).

[29] Section 39 of the Schools Act empowers a School Governing Body of a public school to determine the amount of fees to be charged (without prescribing a maximum limit) and to determine equitable criteria and procedures for the total, partial or conditional exemption of parents who are unable to pay school fees. To illustrate, in 2017 the annual fees for the best performing public school in South Africa is R40,000 (approximately £2,500) per child.

and poorly resourced.[30] This is not the only way in which governing bodies limit access to schools, however. Language policies, admissions criteria, fees and various codes of conduct – including school pregnancy policies – together play a determinative role in defining who gets in, who stays in and who can never get in.

As a justification for wielding their wide statutory powers, school governing bodies draw their qualified democratic legitimacy from their composition. They are composed of elected members of various constituencies directly part of the school at a particular point in time, with parents holding the majority of the available positions, followed by teachers, the provincial department of education and students. In reality, the school governing bodies are not necessarily representative of people who live in the community. Members of the broader community do not participate in the election of a school governing body. Only those who are already part of the school at a particular point in time are eligible to participate in a particular school's governance system. Indeed, demand for quality public schools shows that an increasing number of students do not attend school in their community and travel to better schools in neighbourhoods further away. This further challenges the presumption that school governing bodies reflect the composition of the broader communities in which they are located.

At wealthy, former white, public schools these elected bodies, with their limited franchise, tend in practice to act as gatekeepers at the 'doors of learning', purporting to represent both the internal and broader community within which a school is located.[31] As the cases illustrate, through admissions criteria, language policies and codes of conduct, school governing bodies wield substantial power in determining who has access to education within a given community. It is this contestation, over who is in and who is out, that has been the subject of litigation all the way to the Constitutional Court. In contrast to the second stream of litigation for education inputs which has been

---

[30] Franklin and McLaren, *Realising the right to basic education in South Africa*, at 20. Public schools in South Africa are ranked in a quintile system according to the socioeconomic status of the surrounding communities; the poorest schools rank 1 and the wealthiest rank 5. Under this system, the state provides more non-personnel funding to schools serving poor communities to compensate them for revenue they do not collect through school fees. In 2006, the Department of Education declared all quintile 1 and 2 schools to be 'no-fee schools', meaning they were prohibited from charging compulsory school fees.

[31] E. Fiske and H. Ladd, 'Educational aspirations and political realities', in *Elusive Equity: Education Reform in Post-Apartheid South Africa* at 69, www.jstor.org/stable/10.7864/j.ctt1287bc0.8.

led by civil society organisations seeking to develop a robust right to basic education, wealthy school governing bodies have led the charge to maintain control over public education resources.

In *Hoërskool Ermelo*, the Constitutional Court considered whether the provincial government, acting through the Head of Department (HoD), had the power to revoke a school governing body's determination of its language policy, which stipulated Afrikaans as the only medium of instruction. Bishop's chapter in this volume canvasses the many challenges raised by language rights in realising the right to education in South Africa. The governing body in this case refused to modify its policy and allow English instruction in order to accommodate and include Black African students from the neighbouring township, who were formally receiving education in English and presumably were not well equipped to learn in an Afrikaans medium of instruction for the first time.[32] This was notwithstanding repeated requests from the HoD to do so. The continued refusal of the governing body to change their language policy resulted in the HoD's arguably heavy-handed revocation of the governing body's powers. Although this dispute was framed as a question of authority to set policies, it was underpinned by issues of race and class, as the effect of the policy was to exclude Black children from accessing education, the former an expressly prohibited ground of discrimination under the Constitution.[33]

The Constitutional Court held that the governing body's power to determine a school's language policy is subject to the Constitution and therefore must be understood within the broader constitutional scheme, in order to make education available and accessible to everyone. In ordering the school to review its language policy, the Court emphasised that a governing body does not exclusively serve the school's current students. Rather:

> Their fiduciary duty, then, is to the institution as a dynamic part of an evolving society. The governing body of a public school must in addition recognise that it is entrusted with a public resource which must be managed not only in the interests of those who happen to be students and parents at the time but also in the interests of the broader community

[32] *Hoërskool Ermelo*. At the beginning of 2006, the department approached the school requesting that it admit 27 grade 8 learners who could not be accommodated at any of the English-medium schools in Ermelo because they were already full to capacity.
[33] Section 9(3) and (5) of the Constitution.

in which the school is located and in the light of the values of our Constitution.[34]

However, this statement does not sufficiently wrestle with the limited franchise of school governing bodies discussed above and how their interests can and often do conflict with those of the 'broader community', as *Hoërskool Ermelo* highlights.

The case of *Rivonia* was also concerned with the allocation of powers between a governing body and the provincial education department.[35] This time, the affluent public school claimed that it had reached its admission capacity, being 24 students per grade 1 class and declined to admit the child. But the HoD took a different view, and summarily withdrew the principal's admission function and forcefully placed the child in the school. Soon thereafter, the governing body instituted litigation contending that it had the exclusive power to determine the school's maximum capacity.[36] In the first round, the department's power to determine the maximum capacity of a public school in the Gauteng Province was upheld.[37] However, the Supreme Court of Appeal overturned that decision, reasoning that once the governing body adopted its admission policy, the HoD exercised their powers in accordance with the policy. The Supreme Court of Appeal held that the HoD did not have the power to ride roughshod over the policies of the governing body.[38] It also noted that the governing body was entitled to determine a school's capacity because of the supplementary financial resources raised by the parent body, through fees in particular.[39] The problematic import of this statement highlighted the kernel of the power contestation – control over a crucial public resource – which the Constitutional Court faced frontally in the subsequent appeal. It affirmed the provincial department's role as the bearer of the ultimate power to implement admission decisions.[40] The Court nevertheless set

[34] Hoerskool Ermelo at para. 80.
[35] *MEC for Education in Gauteng Province and Other v Governing Body of Rivonia Primary School and Others* 2013 (6) SA 582 (CC) (henceforth *Rivonia*). See also *Centre for Child Law v The Governing Body of Hoerskool Fochville* 2016 (2) SA 121 (SCA).
[36] *Rivonia*, at para. 2.
[37] *Governing Body of the Rivonia Primary School and Another v MEC for Education: Gauteng Province and Others* [2012] 1 All SA 576 (GSJ).
[38] *Governing Body of the Rivonia Primary School and Another v MEC for Education: Gauteng Province and Others*, at para. 50.
[39] *Governing Body of the Rivonia Primary School and Another v MEC for Education: Gauteng Province and Others*, at para. 29.
[40] *Governing Body of the Rivonia Primary School and Another v MEC for Education: Gauteng Province and Others*, at para. 52.

aside the HoD's interference because it did not act in a procedurally fair manner when revoking the principal's functions. As in *Hoërskool Ermelo* on the issue of a school's language policy, *Rivonia* illustrates that the veneer of democratic legitimacy and the formal participatory mechanism of the school governing body are not sufficient safeguards to protect the interests of the external 'broader community' who have equally legitimate claims to quality education as those inside the school.[41]

In *Welkom*, the Constitutional Court once again confronted the power dynamics between school governing bodies and provincial officials responsible for ensuring that children are able to access school.[42] This time, governing bodies from two schools imposed their respective pregnancy policies on girl-students by forcing them to leave school while pregnant and remain out of school for a year after giving birth. In response to these measures taken by the governing bodies, the HoD of the province instructed the respective principals to disregard the governing bodies' policies and readmit the students, thus recognising the blatant interferences in the girls' right to a basic education. The school governing bodies retaliated by seeking an order from the High Court to stop the HoD from intervening, on the basis that the public authority failed to act procedurally fairly.

Although the constitutionality of the offending policies was not in issue, the Constitutional Court accepted that the pregnancy policies violated the students' rights to human dignity, equality and basic education.[43] Consequently, it ordered the school governing bodies to review their pregnancy policies in the light of the Constitution. As Fredman observes, instead of dealing head on with the substantive protection of the rights of vulnerable female students, the Constitutional Court deferred to the school governing body and 'left open the possibility that the schools' actions might be justified in proper proceedings'.[44]

Each of the cases discussed above was instituted by governing bodies seeking to assert their power in the exercise of control over school resources. However, the cases were not overtly framed in this

---

[41] See S. Fredman, 'Procedure or principle? The role of adjudication in achieving the right to education', *Constitutional Court Review VI* (2014) for an insightful evaluation of the Constitutional Court's approach in *Rivonia*.

[42] *Head of Department, Department of Education, Free State Province v Welkom High School and Another; Head of Department, Department of Education, Free State Province v Harmony High School and Another* 2014 (2) SA 228 (CC) (henceforth Welkom).

[43] Fredman, 'Procedure or principle?', 170.

[44] Fredman, 'Procedure or principle?', 172.

way. Rather, the school governing bodies positioned their claims as a defence against heavy-handed public officials who exercised a public power without due regard to the procedural protections required when public officials perform administrative acts. The officials were required to act fairly and expected not to resort to high-handed decrees even to enforce legitimate claims of students, particularly in the context of South Africa's democratic constitutional framework that so jealously guards the rule of law.[45]

In each of the cases concerning the players and their powers, the central question of law in issue was most appropriately and best resolved in judicial review proceedings, as framed by the governing bodies. However, as we have argued, the cases pivoted on crucial issues of equality, access to education and the protections afforded to vulnerable students. Viewed in this way, the cases also presented opportunities for the courts to consider the powers of schools and government in the context of their impact on the rights to equality and to a basic education.

The *Hoërskool Ermelo* and *Rivonia* Constitutional Court judgments highlight how the approach to school governing bodies' powers to refuse admission based on the school's language or capacity policy determinations impacts the ability of students to gain access to basic education. Significantly, each of the three cases has affirmed that school governing bodies exercise their powers subject to the Constitution and ultimately to the state's duty to ensure that everyone has access to a school. In *Hoërskool Ermelo*, *Rivonia* and *Welkom*, the court recognised the power of school governing bodies to formulate policies relating to language, admissions and pregnancy respectively, but acknowledged in principle the power of provincial government to intervene in appropriate cases, and subject to procedural safeguards, where the Constitution so requires. While these cases bring welcome clarification of the contours of the relative powers at play, the courts have paid insufficient attention to the conflict of interests among the insular school governing bodies, the state and those who are outside of the school. It is generally being left to the parties and friends of the court (*amici curiae*) to ensure that these considerations are properly before the courts by introducing relevant evidence and argument that broadens the scope of the issues. Where this does not happen, the court has the power to invite submissions on particular aspects of the

---

[45] *Economic Freedom Fighters v Speaker of the National Assembly and Others; Democratic Alliance v Speaker of the National Assembly and Others* 2016 (3) SA 580 (CC) at para. 1.

case that are not frontally raised by the parties but which are relevant to the issues before it.[46]

In *Hoërskool Ermelo*, *Rivonia* and *Welkom*, the Constitutional Court did seek to strike a balance between the rule of law concerns underpinning the exercise of policy-making powers and the impact of those powers on the rights to a basic education and equality. This set of cases confirms that education departments must take an assertive approach in mediating these contestations through appropriate regulatory or policy guidance, instead of leaving it up to the school governing bodies or the courts to resolve. This is most pointedly highlighted in Deputy Chief Justice Moseneke's last judgment in *FEDSAS* (quoted at the beginning of this chapter), in which the Constitutional Court upheld provincial regulations aimed at giving the provincial education department a greater role in determining admission to schools in the province. Importantly the Court recognised that the parochial interests of school governing bodies must be tempered by the higher norm of securing 'universal and non-discriminatory access to education'.[47] But even more fundamentally, the Constitutional Court held that wealthier schools, offering high standards of education, can be compelled by law to make education available in a manner that is consistent with the state's broader objectives.

Blackboards, books and buildings: litigating education 'inputs'

In the previous section, we reviewed litigation relating to who gets to determine policy on key aspects of public education, including admissions, language and pregnancy. In this section, we are primarily concerned with a determination of the 'inputs' that are necessary to exercise the right to a basic education. After having discussed the question of 'who is in and who is out?' in the previous section, this section will focus on *what* exactly it is that students in public schools are guaranteed, as a part of the right to a basic education. It is in relation to these issues that South Africa has most recently seen a spate of public interest litigation, as well as other forms of campaigning.

---

[46] Notably, in *KwaZulu-Natal Joint Liaison Committee v MEC Department of Education, Kwazulu-Natal and Others*, the Constitutional Court invited the parties to make further written submissions after the oral hearing on the basis for enforcing the applicant's claim.

[47] *Federation of Governing Bodies for South African Schools (FEDSAS) v Member of the Executive Council for Education, Gauteng and Another*, para. 44.

Local communities and grassroots organisations, for instance, have mobilised to enforce the right to a basic education most vocally and effectively over the physical conditions of schools. These strategies have included public demonstrations and making submissions to legislative committees in order to contribute to policy making and to comment on government spending on education. In addition, strategic use of the media to highlight the experiences of school children has made the challenges in the education system more widely known, fostering sentiments of moral outrage at the conditions in which millions of children must learn every day.

The flagship litigation conducted initially by the Legal Resources Centre and later the Equal Education Law Centre with regard to the establishment of binding norms and standards for school infrastructure formed a key thrust of a broader campaign by the highly effective social movement, Equal Education.[48] The initial litigation instituted by the Legal Resources Centre resulted in the Minister of Basic Education making new regulations. The new, binding standards provide that all schools must have access to sufficient water, electricity, sanitation, safe classrooms with a maximum of 40 learners, security, internet, libraries, computer and science laboratories, and recreational facilities.[49]

In litigation on more discrete issues, successful cases were brought to secure the appointment of teachers to vacant posts in public schools,[50] the provision of school furniture,[51] textbooks,[52] workbooks and scholar transport.[53] Many of these cases also formed part of broader campaigns by organisations such as Equal Education and local communities. In this section, we consider the cumulative impact of these cases in, first, filling out the content of the right to a basic education in s 29(1)(a)

[48] See www.equaleducation.org.za. Equal Education is a movement of parents, teachers and learners campaigning for quality and equality in the education system. It is registered as a non-governmental organisation in terms of the company laws of South Africa and is dependent on donor funding and donations from the public.

[49] Open Society Justice Initiative, *Equal Access to Quality Education*, New York: Open Society Foundation, 2017, at 64–5.

[50] *Centre for Child Law v Minister of Basic Education* 2013 (3) SA 183 (ECG); *Linkside and Others v Minister of Basic Education and Others* [2015] ZAECGHC 36.

[51] *Madzodzo and Others v Minister of Basic Education and Others* 2014 (3) SA 441 (ECM).

[52] *Minister of Basic Education v Basic Education for All* [2016] 1 All SA 369 (SCA); 2016 (4) SA 63 (SCA); *Section 27 and Others v Minister of Education and Another* 2013 (2) SA 40 (GNP). For an excellent account and analysis of the textbooks litigation in Limpopo, see Faranaaz Veriava, 'The Limpopo textbook litigation: a case study into the possibilities of a transformative constitutionalism', *South African Journal of Human Rights*, 32 (2016): 321–43.

[53] *Tripartite Steering Committee v Minister of Basic Education* 2015 (5) SA 107 (ECG).

of the South African Constitution and, second, developing novel and creative legal remedies to give effect to it.

The Legal Resources Centre and Centre for Child Law were the primary legal players in early cases on education provisioning, acting on behalf of students and schools in the Eastern Cape Province. More recently, the public interest law organisation SECTION27 has led litigation on provisioning of textbooks in Limpopo Province and Equal Education's legal arm, the Equal Education Law Centre, has taken up cases on school infrastructure, scholar transport and discrimination in schools.[54]

South Africa is divided into nine geographic provinces, each of which has unique features in its history, language, economy and natural resources. It is pertinent to note that the Eastern Cape and Limpopo, former 'Homelands' reserved for Africans who were denied citizenship rights in South Africa, are among the poorest provinces, and have arguably the worst performing education departments.[55] The collapse of the education departments in these two provinces prompted the national executive to exercise its powers to intervene in the provinces and assume their functions, under section 100 of the Constitution.[56] The courts recognised, in these cases, that the inadequate and unequal education in many parts of South Africa is one of the legacies of apartheid.

As Roberson J observed in *Linkside*:

> In 1994 the Eastern Cape province inherited an unequal education system which included under-funded and under-resourced schools in the poor former homelands.[57]

The cases seeking delivery of necessary inputs for education have incrementally fleshed out the content of the right to a basic education. The High Court confirmed that the content of the right includes, at the very least, the provision of teachers[58] and non-educator staff[59] and

---

[54] See: www.equaleducationlawcentre.org.za.
[55] Franklin and McLaren, *Realising the right to basic education in South Africa*.
[56] *Minister of Basic Education v Basic Education for All*, para. 5 (in respect of Limpopo); *Centre for Child Law v Minister of Basic Education*, paras. 4–8 (in respect of the Eastern Cape).
[57] *Linkside and Others v Minister of Basic Education and Others*, para. 5.
[58] *Centre for Child Law v Minister of Basic Education*, para. 1 and the order at para. 35; *Linkside and Others v Minister of Basic Education and Others*, paras. 24–6.
[59] *Centre for Child Law v Minister of Basic Education*, paras. 21 and 32–4.

each of the following inputs – a place to read and write (furniture),[60] textbooks[61] and scholar transport[62] and – through a series of settlements – adequate classrooms and school buildings. This body of cases has therefore substantially developed the content of the right.

The approach of the courts, in each of these cases, has been to focus on the *impact* of the absence of the specific 'input' that was at issue – such as teachers or textbooks. The courts thus ask: what is the impact of the absence of these inputs on a learner and on the learning process? In light of this, Plasket J in *Tripartite Steering Committee v Minister of Basic Education* noted that many students in the Eastern Cape had to walk long distances, often at risk to their safety:

> The result is that a great burden, both physical and psychological, is placed on scholars who are required to walk long distances to school. They are often required to wake extremely early, and only get home late.[63]

In *Madzodzo*, dealing with school furniture, Goosen J similarly held that:

> It is clear from the evidence presented by the applicants that inadequate resources in the form of insufficient or inappropriate desks and chairs in the classrooms in public schools across the province profoundly undermines the right of access to basic education.[64]

The Court quotes from the affidavit evidence describing in concrete terms the impact of a lack of school furniture on students, including that students are forced to share desks, are unable to write in class, have to sit on bricks, crates or plastic chairs that they bring with them to school, and that this creates discipline problems and results in an environment not conducive to teaching and learning.[65] The court in each case also identified how all of the components of the right are linked with one another, cumulatively creating a

---

[60] *Madzodzo and Others v Minister of Basic Education and Others*, paras. 20–1.
[61] *Minister of Basic Education v Basic Education for All*, para. 42 and Section 27 and Others v Minister of Education and Another, para. 25.
[62] *Tripartite Steering Committee v Minister of Basic Education*, para. 14.
[63] *Tripartite Steering Committee v Minister of Basic Education*, para. 14.
[64] *Madzodzo and Others v Minister of Basic Education and Others*, para. 20.
[65] *Madzodzo and Others v Minister of Basic Education and Others*, para. 20.

conducive environment in which teaching and learning may take place. In *Tripartite Steering Committee*, Plasket J explained that:

> The right to education is meaningless without teachers to teach, administrators to keep schools running, desks and other furniture to allow scholars to do their work, textbooks from which to learn and transport to and from school at state expense in appropriate cases.[66]

At the heart of this conception of the right to education is the idea that, in order to satisfy the Constitution, education must be fit for purpose. Thus, merely adding up the individual components does not make up the right to education without an adequate vision of the nature and purpose of the right to a basic education. The courts do *not* accept that formal enrolment and attendance are sufficient.[67] Instead, as they consider whether certain inputs or resources form part of the content of the right, they require that the actual substance of education serve the purpose of effective learning and teaching to empower students to participate in society as active citizens and access opportunities after completing their schooling.[68]

In the course of developing the content of a right to basic education, litigators and the courts have also innovated to develop new and creative remedies. The procedural dimension of these cases, in particular the approach to remedies, has a number of interesting features. First, the cases saw an unusually high degree of orders by consent of the state respondents or settlement agreements, in particular on the substantive rights and obligations in issue. Second, the cases were conducted in a multi-stage or 'serialised' manner, combining a number of elements that resulted in multi-layer complex structural orders from the courts. Third, the courts employed a number of novel orders, such as 'deeming orders' and class actions. We discuss these remedial dimensions of the litigation below.

The first noteworthy feature of the litigation regarding education infrastructure, in comparison to other socioeconomic rights litigation

---

[66] *Tripartite Steering Committee v Minister of Basic Education*, para. 14. See also *Madzodzo and Others v Minister of Basic Education and Others*, para. 19.

[67] *Madzodzo and Others v Minister of Basic Education and Others*, para. 20, holding that '[t]he state's obligation to provide basic education as guaranteed by the Constitution is not confined to making places available at schools. It necessarily requires the provision of a range of educational resources: – schools, classrooms, teachers, teaching materials and appropriate facilities for learners.'

[68] *Madzodzo and Others v Minister of Basic Education and Others*, paras. 18–19.

in South Africa, is the high frequency of consent orders and settlement agreements. Two of the major cases, the 'mud schools' litigation and the 'norms and standards' case, were, at least initially, entirely resolved by agreement among the parties. The state respondents effectively accepted their constitutional responsibilities and committed to taking the necessary steps to eradicate unsafe schools in the Eastern Cape and to adopt legally binding regulations governing school infrastructure, respectively.[69] Even in those cases that ultimately resulted in judgments, the state frequently consented to a portion of the relief.[70] In particular, the state conceded, either expressly or by its conduct, that the right to education entitled students to what was claimed (furniture,[71] teachers,[72] textbooks[73] or scholar transport[74]) and undertook in principle to remedy the rights violations. What remained to be argued was generally the scope and nature of the remaining relief. Thus, unlike in the litigation concerning the powers to determine policy discussed above, there was generally no dispute concerning what the right to a basic education required the state to provide, in terms of tangible 'inputs'. The disputes in these cases related to implementation and remedies.

The second distinguishing feature of the remedial aspects of this body of jurisprudence is that most of the cases involved serialised litigation, that is, there were few one-off cases, and as a result there are complex structural orders. In most of the cases that we discuss in this section, the litigation involved three or more hearings and court orders, with the orders becoming more detailed, complex and prescriptive as the proceedings developed. The litigation took place in multiple stages, in some instances because it was planned that way by the litigators driving

---

[69] C. McConnachie and C. McConnachie, 'Concretising the right to a basic education', *South African Law Journal*, 129(3) (2012): 554.

[70] *Madzodzo and Others v Minister of Basic Education and Others*, paras. 3 and 8; *Centre for Child Law v Minister of Basic Education*, para. 9.

[71] *Madzodzo and Others v Minister of Basic Education and Others*, para. 21.

[72] *Centre for Child Law v Minister of Basic Education*, para. 9.

[73] *Minister of Basic Education v Basic Education for All*, para. 42, where the SCA held that government itself, through its policy and actions, had given content to the right to a basic education by committing to provide a textbook for each learner in each grade. However, we note that the state disputed the proposition that the right to a basic education entitled each child to every prescribed textbook.

[74] *Tripartite Steering Committee v Minister of Basic Education*, referring to the government policy adopted to give effect to the right to scholar transport.

it and in others because the subsequent phases were responses to non-compliance with earlier orders.[75] We discuss some examples below.

The effect of conducting the litigation in stages was to enable the litigants to establish the content of the right and the obligations of the state in principle; to secure a basic order requiring provision of the necessary resource; to create a supervisory framework for the implementation of the order and to refine that framework to secure compliance; and thereby to 'scale up' the relief, moving from individual schools in the first stage to an entire province by the end. The litigation by the Legal Resources Centre to secure school furniture and the appointment and payment of teachers on behalf of schools and students in the Eastern Cape are good examples of how this process played out in serial litigation.

The first example of the multi-stage nature of this litigation is seen in the furniture case, *Madzodzo*. The final reported judgment in *Madzodzo* records that there had been two previous orders made (by consent) before the matter was argued before Goosen J. The first order identified that the lack of furniture in schools was a breach of the education right. The Court directed the provincial department to conduct an audit of school furniture needs in the province, appoint a Furniture Task Team, and publish a circular to inform schools of the process and to endeavour to meet the furniture needs identified by this process before a specified deadline.[76] The provincial department failed to meet its commitment to deliver furniture by the deadline and concerns also emerged that the audit of needs was incomplete. This prompted a return to court. In the second phase of litigation, a second order was made in terms of which additional schools (previously omitted from the process) were added, an independent body was appointed to verify the findings of the department's audit and a fresh deadline was set for delivery of furniture.[77]

A second example of how this litigation ran in stages is seen in the cases dealing with teachers in the Eastern Cape. The litigation to secure the appointment of teachers to vacant posts and to secure payment of their salaries had a series of sequels, each building on the first case. The first stage produced the judgment in *Centre for Child Law*, which confirmed that the state was required to fill vacancies and

---

[75] Jason Brickhill was one of the counsel for the applicants in stages of *Madzodzo; Centre for Child Law; Tripartite Steering Committee; Linkside* and in the initial stage of Equal Education's 'norms and standards' litigation.

[76] *Madzodzo and Others v Minister of Basic Education and Others*, paras. 3–6.

[77] *Madzodzo and Others v Minister of Basic Education and Others*, paras. 7–8.

to pay teachers, and set out a series of steps it was required to do to achieve this. When the state failed to comply, the Legal Resources Centre instituted the proceedings which, after several orders by consent, resulted in the judgment in *Linkside*. The court in *Linkside* certified an opt-in class action, enabling affected schools to opt into the class to secure the appointment and payment of teachers. In the end, over 120 schools benefited, although it is likely that other schools remained unaware of the litigation and were unable to participate, especially the poorest schools in remote rural areas. The Court also ordered the appointment of a claims administrator, who was responsible for receiving and processing claims including dispensing funds to schools that had paid teachers who ought to have been paid by government.

Some of the specific orders granted in these cases were also remarkable in other respects, quite apart from the serialised nature of the litigation discussed above. Perhaps the most radical remedies granted in any among this set of cases were seen in *Linkside*, regarding teacher appointments and payment. This case was the first class action in any area of law to be 'certified' by the High Court in South Africa following the development by the courts of new procedural rules to govern class actions.[78] In that respect, *Linkside* already broke substantial new ground in the law of class actions. However, on the merits, two other aspects of the eventual order were notable. The first of these was that the Court appointed a claims administrator, being a firm of chartered accountants, to administer the claims by schools for unpaid teacher salaries and to dispense the funds to claimant schools. The Court cited a recent Supreme Court of Appeal decision that had recommended the use of novel remedies such as the appointment of a 'special master', a mechanism used relatively frequently in the United States of America. Second, the Court gave a novel 'deeming' order that kicked in when the provincial department failed to appoint a teacher to a vacant post following demand by the school. In those circumstances, the teacher who had been interviewed and recommended by the school governing bodies would be 'deemed' to have been appointed

---

[78] The rules governing class actions were developed in *Trustees for the time being of Children's Resource Centre Trust and Others v Pioneer Food (Pty) Ltd and Others* 2013 (2) SA 213 (SCA).

by the department.[79] In effect, the litigants anticipated the possibility of non-compliance and requested the Court to exercise judicial remedial powers to perform what would ordinarily be an executive function of appointing teachers, given the systemic failures within the department to act diligently and without delay. These examples provide a powerful illustration of the potential of litigation to dismantle bureaucratic barriers to the provision of resources crucial to the enjoyment of the right to a basic education.

The litigation regarding infrastructure and education resources has been ground-breaking in multiple ways. The jurisprudence has carved out the content of the constitutional right to a basic education, confirming that the right includes the provision of adequate classrooms and buildings, teachers, textbooks, school furniture and scholar transport. This body of cases went even further by developing novel and creative judicial remedies. These include structural interdicts imposing reporting and court supervision, an audit of needs, the appointment of independent bodies to verify needs and to administer claims, 'deeming orders' to enable teacher appointments, and the use of a class action to secure relief for a large number of schools. Although compliance remains imperfect, on their own terms these cases reveal that hundreds of thousands of students have been provided with these components of a basic education in the Eastern Cape and Limpopo provinces.

Conclusion

After a period of relative quiet in relation to education rights litigation following the transition to constitutional democracy in 1994, the last decade has seen section 29 of the Constitution spring to life. In the context of a public education system which is characterised by high levels of inequality and parts of which are in crisis, students, schools and civil society have resorted to the courts. Usually, once an issue presents itself – whether that concerns the political, governance, issues or inadequate physical education inputs – resort to the courts often comes at an early stage. However, in the case of Equal Education's demand

---

[79] *Linkside and Others v Minister of Basic Education and Others*, para. 1, setting out para. 3.3 of the order, which reads: 'It is declared that, in the event that the first respondent and the fourth respondent fail to act on such recommendations of the School Governing Boards within 15 days, the educators will be deemed to have been appointed, in which event the fourth respondent is directed to issue each such educator with a letter of appointment within 10 days thereafter.'

for binding norms and standards for school infrastructure, litigation followed as a last resort after several years of political campaigning.

We have traced the key decisions in relation to two streams of litigation – policy-making powers and educational 'inputs'. The fact that these two streams run largely separately, and are driven by a different set of role-players, is no accident. It is reflective of two parallel systems of education, which produce students with disparate skills and abilities. On the one hand, we see claims to maintain control of existing public resources at better-off schools; and on the other, increasing pressure for provision of the education inputs that are already available at the wealthier, well-provisioned schools. Thus, the first stream of litigation relating to policy-making powers has involved relatively better resourced public schools that were formerly reserved for white students, generally in large urban areas, which have sought to assert power along lines such as language (in the case of *Hoërskool Ermelo*) and school fees (in the case of *Rivonia*). It is these cases that have reached the Constitutional Court in opposition to the state's attempts to protect the rights of learners (as was the case in *Welkom* concerning student pregnancy) and draw wealthier schools into the communal pot of state resources to be used to improve access to education for everyone. All the while, a growing number of cases concerning education inputs in the lower courts are advancing the education right for the majority of learners in the poorest schools.

In respect of the power to determine key school policies, the Constitutional Court has sought to strike a balance between recognising the democratic and community-level legitimacy of school governing bodies, on one hand, and the need to empower government to act in the interests of *all* students and to promote equal education, on the other. The intervention power of government is a vital check on school governing bodies, which otherwise have the potential to reinforce and reproduce patterns of inequality that characterise the South African education system as a whole. The Court also emphasised the need for all the role-players to collaborate constructively in the interests of *all* students, not merely those who happen to already be enrolled at the relevant school, and to act consistently with the Constitution.

In the second category of cases, mostly decided in the High Court, the courts incrementally developed the content of the right to a basic education in section 29(1)(a). The right includes, at the very least, the provision of teachers and non-educator staff, and each of the following inputs – a place to read and write (furniture), textbooks and scholar transport, and – through a series of settlements – adequate classrooms and school buildings. The courts also engaged in remedial innovations, developing complex structural orders. These included orders requiring government reporting and court supervision, an audit of school needs, the appointment of independent bodies to verify needs and to administer claims, 'deeming orders' to enable teacher appointments, and the use of a class action to secure relief for a large number of schools. The serialised nature of these cases demonstrates that, more often than not, the direct outcome of litigation does not achieve an immediate or self-executing solution. It requires constant monitoring and pressure. In that regard structural interdicts that prescribe time lines are important tools.

This lesson regarding the need to approach public interest litigation flexibly and creatively, focusing on the actual impact, emerges strongly from both categories of cases. In the 'powers' cases, the message of the Constitutional Court is clear: in the tussle for the power to determine policy, the focus of all the role-players must be on the rights of the students and the aspirations of the constitutional framework to secure a quality education for all. In the cases dealing with infrastructure and resources, the courts have given content to the right within a vision of education as an empowerment right.

Public interest litigation on the right to a basic education is not an end in itself. But developing a cohesive framework for policy formulation and giving substantive content to the constitutional right provide a platform from which communities and social movements may press the political claim for equal access to quality education. And the court process provides increased opportunities for engagement and collaboration between the state and school communities, and the potential to undo bureaucratic blockages and channel state resources to schools and students in desperate need.

TEN

Human rights and equality in education: Conclusion

Sandra Fredman, Meghan Campbell and Helen Taylor

This collection of essays has explored a range of challenges faced by minorities and disadvantaged groups in education. The book demonstrates how a human rights-based approach brings these challenges into sharper focus and offers a framework for addressing them so that we can achieve quality education for all. These insights are enriched through the comparative perspective provided by the range of jurisdictions featured in the collection. Such a perspective highlights the complexity of the challenges faced and presents contextualised responses to them. Human rights provide a common language to share and compare the experiences of minorities and disadvantaged groups in education. While requiring sensitive attention to be given to how these experiences are embedded in particular contexts, a comparative perspective also enables resonances to be felt across contextual divides. It is therefore capable of inspiring new ideas for overcoming long-standing challenges in education.

An increasingly pressing challenge faced by a human rights-based approach, covered in Part I of this collection, is the question of how to hold actors other than the state accountable for providing quality education to all. While remaining open to the potential benefits of private educational initiatives for disadvantaged and marginalised children who might lose out in the public school system (Smuts), the accountability deficit associated with the involvement of private actors in education needs to be addressed. This accountability deficit leaves minorities and disadvantaged groups most at risk that their right to education will not be realised, and the challenge moving forward is to develop robust accountability mechanisms for ensuring both the state and private actors uphold children's rights to and in education (O'Mahony).

Part II emphasised the importance of sensitive balancing of competing rights and interests in education, particularly with respect to the tension that often arises between the right to education and the freedom of religion and culture. An especially important insight offered by both chapters in Part II is that this balancing exercise requires acute awareness of the contextual and historical positioning of minority groups within the education system. While a human rights-based approach calls for protections to be extended to minorities and disadvantaged groups to ensure they are not marginalised by the education system, we should remain alert to such protections being subverted by groups seeking minority status in order to exclude other groups (Kothari) or being abused in order to preserve historical privilege or restrict access to education (Bishop). A human rights-based approach throws these tensions into sharp relief, but further work needs to done to ensure that these protections empower minority and disadvantaged groups and so unlock the transformative potential of education.

While there have been significant victories for gender equality in education, particularly as we inch closer to achieving universal access to education, Part III called for attention to be given to other gender inequalities that stand in the way of boys and girls enjoying equal rights in education. The principle of substantive equality facilitates a rich evaluation of progress towards equality in education (Fredman) as it sets out four mutually enhancing dimensions of equality: (1) redressing disadvantage; (2) addressing stigma, stereotyping, prejudice and violence; (3) facilitating participation; and (4) accommodating difference and achieving structural change. These dimensions are clearly evident when examining how the content, structure and delivery of sex education, as one component of education provision, can perpetuate and reinforce gender inequalities (Campbell). Much work still remains for a human rights-based approach in using the principle of substantive equality to shine the spotlight on other forms of gender inequality in education.

Part IV brought the collection to a close by illustrating both the risks and the potential benefits of leveraging courts to enforce the right to education. The strength of a human rights-based assessment of quality lies in its insistence that education provision is a positive human rights duty that the state is obliged to fulfil rather than simply a distributive decision left to the unfettered discretion of policy makers (Taylor). It illustrates the strategic benefit of relying on quality or adequacy in education litigation, the challenge remains as to how the state can be held accountable for complying with their human rights obligation to deliver quality education. The two distinct streams of education jurisprudence which have emerged in South Africa demonstrate, on the one hand, that strategic litigation can secure concrete relief in form of basic facilities and resources for children and schools that the public education system is failing, but runs the risk, on the other hand, that wealthier schools can exploit their easier access to court to protect their privilege and control over a disproportionate share of public resources (Brickhill and van Leeve). While litigation can be a very effective tool for enforcing children's human rights in education, it is important to look beyond the courtroom to the impact that litigation has in the classroom and ensure it is complemented by other strategies for improving education provision for the most disadvantaged children and schools.

A human rights-based approach to education offers a promising framework for identifying and addressing the obstacles that stand in the way of minorities and disadvantaged groups enjoying equal rights to quality education. It should serve as a blueprint for laws, policies and programmes geared towards achieving Sustainable Development Goal 4 – universal access to quality education. The diversity of perspectives featured in this collection consider these obstacles from a variety of viewpoints, illuminating more fully the complexities that need to be considered in order to successfully overcome them. We need to continue these conversations across countries in a way that brings together all the actors and stakeholders in the education system to work in partnership towards a rights-oriented vision of quality education for all children.

Index